BEDE COLLEGE

D0293482

338.5
STANDARD

STUDIES IN ECON S

Markets and Market Failure

Stephen Munday

BEDE SIXTH FORM
B003280

Series Editor
Susan Grant
West Oxfordshire College

Heinemann

43395010030984427726012

Heinemann Educational Publishers
Halley Court, Jordan Hill, Oxford OX2 8EJ
a division of Reed Educational & Professional Publishing Ltd

OXFORD   MELBOURNE   AUCKLAND
JOHANNESBURG   BLANTYRE   GABORONE
IBADAN   PORTSMOUTH (NH) USA   CHICAGO

Heinemann is a registered trademark of Reed Educational & Professional Publishing Ltd

Text © Stephen Munday, 2000

First published in 2000

04 03 02 01
9 8 7 6 5 4 3 2

All rights reserved.

British Library Cataloguing in Publication Data
A catalogue record for this book is available from the British Library

ISBN 0 435 33050 0

Typeset by Wyvern 21 Ltd
Printed and bound in Great Britain by Biddles Ltd, Guildford

Acknowledgements
The publishers would like to thank the following for permission to reproduce copyright
material: OCR exam questions on pages, 8, 15, 48, 59, 78, 91 and 104 reproduced with
permission of OCR Examinations; Edexcel exam questions on pages 91, 104 and 119
reproduced with permisson of Edexcel Foundation; Pg 5 pie charts from 'Pre-budget report:
a summary leaflet', HM Treasury, November 1999; Pg 12, 53, 75, 88, 105, 108 and 112
extracts from 'The Independent'; Pg 16 graphs from 'The Guardian', 3/12/1996; Pg 17 pie
charts from 'The Financial Mail on Sunday', 17/3/1996 © Atlantic Syndication Partners;
Pg 22 table from Social Trends 29, 1999', Office of National Statistics. © Crown Copyright
2000; Pg 26, 52 and 117 extracts from 'The Economist' © The Economist; Pg 27 table
from 'The World Development Report', Oxford University Press, Inc., 1992; Pg 28 table
from 'Annual Abstract of Statistics' (1995), and graph from 'Social Trends 26' (1996),
Office of National Statistics © Crown Copyright 2000; Pg 30 extract by Jeremy Atiyah,
from 'The Independent on Sunday', 14/11/1999; Pg 38, 45, 61, 65, 72, 74, 80, 86, 89, 98
and 116 reproduced with permission of 'The Daily Telegraph'; Pg 41 extract from Reuters,
1/3/2000; Pg 55 extract from 'The Daily Mirror', 23/12/1999; Pg 100 extract from 'PR
Newswire, Washington', 14/12/1999. Used with permission of PR Newswire and The Pew
Center on Global Climate Change; Pg 102 extract from 'News Unlimited', 17/12/1999;
Pg 106 graph, Office of National Statistics © Crown Copyright 2000; Pg 120 extract
adapted from Patrick Minsford, 'Economic Affairs', October to November 1998.

The publishers have made every effort to contact copyright holders. However, if any
material has been incorrectly acknowledged, the publishers would be pleased to correct this
at the earliest opportunity

Tel: 01865 888058 www.heinemann.co.uk

Contents

Preface

This new book in the SEB series is written by Stephen Munday – an experienced writer, teacher and Principal Examiner for the AS Market Failure and Government Intervention papers. He has also recently been involved in the development of the new Advanced Subsidiary and Advanced Specifications in Economics.

Stephen always writes in a very lucid and easily accessible style. This book is no exception. Throughout Stephen relates economic theory to current day issues and makes economic concepts involved very easy to understand.

The book covers the workings of markets, market failure, the effects of government intervention and examines the issues of the environment and health care.

Susan Grant
Series Editor

Introduction

Economics is an exciting subject when it combines theory with application. Economic theory may have interest in its own right. However, the interest in the study of the subject is greatly heightened when the theory studied can be appropriately applied to significant issues of the day. A study of economics can then give us a real insight into and understanding of some of those major issues and a view of the possible approaches that may or may not be appropriate for governments to take.

This mixing of economic theory with application to contemporary issues is nowhere clearer than in the area of markets, market failure and government intervention. It is the focus of this book. How are we to understand the fundamental concerns we have about the environment, our system of health care, our transport network and our education system? What sorts of policies could the government reasonably attempt in these areas? Why do governments so often seem to make mistakes when they attempt policies on these and other issues? An understanding of markets and market failure (and government failure) can give us a real insight into these issues. There is clear economic theory that can be appropriately applied to major current areas of concern.

Chapter 1 clarifies the fundamental problem of scarce resources and infinite wants at the heart of the subject. This implies that opportunity cost exists and this and related concepts are shown on the production possibility frontier. All types of economy have to work out how best to resolve this basic economic problem.

Chapter 2 examines the important concept of economic efficiency. Economists have a clear meaning for this term that is all to do with making the best use of scarce economic resources. It is vital that this is understood properly so that judgements can be made about how good or bad a job markets and governments can be seen to do.

Chapter 3 looks at the arguments that have been expressed since the time of Adam Smith that markets can work wonderfully well to deliver the best possible use of resources and hence deliver economic efficiency. If markets work well, they should simply be left to get on with things. 'Laissez-faire' rules.

Chapter 4 points out the various different reasons why markets may not work as well as suggested in chapter 3. In other words, it looks at why markets may fail: they may not lead to economic efficiency. A proper understanding of the concepts in this chapter is central to a proper understanding of this whole area of economic theory and its possible application.

Chapter 5 considers the concept of equity. This represents a further possible concern about markets, namely that they may result in inequity. The chapter also points out the traditional difficulty of economics with this area: it involves some clear value judgements.

Chapter 6 takes the concerns of chapters 4 and 5 and suggests the different sorts of government policies that could be used to try to overcome the perceived problems with markets. As with chapter 4, this is a central chapter to a full understanding of this area of economics. It represents the key point of application: what could governments reasonably try to do to improve resource allocation?

Chapter 7 makes the vital point that just because markets fail, there cannot be an automatic presumption that governments will do any better. Governments also have problems that cause their policies to lead to less than ideal allocations of scarce resources.

Chapter 8 takes the economics of the first seven chapters and applies it to an area of fundamental concern to societies today: the environment. The suggestion of this chapter is that the problems are essentially economic ones and that a study of relevant economic theory can greatly aid our understanding here. It can help to devise appropriate government policies to try to combat the concerns.

Chapter 9 examines the difficult issue of the provision of health care in today's society. Why do we appear to spend ever more and yet appear to be increasingly dissatisfied with the service provided? Has our current type of provision had its day? Is the solution simply to spend far more than we currently do? Can the private sector help or will it make things worse? These are all issues to do with markets, market failures and government intervention.

Chapter One

Choice and the allocation of resources

'The first lesson of economics is scarcity: there is never enough of anything to fully satisfy those who want it. The first lesson of politics is to disregard the first lesson of economics.'
Thomas Sowell

The nature of economics

- How should we define the subject of **economics**?
- What is it that provides a subject called 'Economics' with a distinct area of study?
- What frames the content for study within economics?

These are vital questions to be answered by anyone who is embarking upon a study of economics. Fortunately, economists have a clear and agreed answer to these questions. Economics is the study of how individuals and societies attempt to use the **scarce resources** available to them to try to meet their **infinite wants**. There is no limit to what we all might, in theory, like to do and achieve. However, there is a clear limit to the resources that are available to us with which to try to achieve all those desires. These resources (known as the **factors of production**) are placed into four categories in economics:

- Land. All natural resources.
- Labour. All human effort available for production.
- Capital. All human-made forms of production.
- Enterprise. The human force that takes the risk and puts the other factors of production to work in order to produce goods and services.

Thus, at the heart of the study of economics is a problem. We have to make, often difficult, decisions about how to allocate our scarce resources between the many competing calls upon those resources. Economics is thus all about decision-making. **Choices** have to be made about the best **allocation of resources**.

Opportunity cost

Stemming from the basic economic problem is the key economic concept of **opportunity cost**. As we cannot have all that we might want (due to the scarcity of resources available to us) then we have to make difficult decisions about what to produce and consume. Inevitably such decisions imply implicit decisions about the things that we must sacrifice or forego. This is the essence of opportunity cost.

The opportunity cost of something is the *next best alternative that is foregone by having or doing that thing*. The whole of life is full of such opportunity costs:

- If I buy a chocolate bar, my opportunity cost is the packet of peppermints that was my other possible choice with the money in my pocket.
- If a farmer uses a field to grow wheat then he or she cannot use that field to grow rape seed (the other crop under consideration).
- If the government spends some tax revenue on building a new hospital then it is not possible to build three new schools (a possible alternative). All government spending decisions can be seen in this way. The figures for spending on different categories by the government all have an opportunity cost. All the money spent in every area could have had an alternative use and thus has an opportunity cost. The £61 billion spent on health care could have been used in any of the other ways shown in the extract from the Pre-Budget Report.

The list can be endless with regard both to large and small decisions and to decisions about production and consumption.

The production possibility frontier

A further way of understanding the use of scarce resources to produce products to meet infinite wants and the related idea of opportunity cost is through the **production possibility frontier**. The production possibility frontier shows the *combinations of products that can be produced given the resources that are available*.

A production possibility frontier is usually used to illustrate the production potential of a national economy. However, it could equally well be used to consider the production capability of a firm or even an individual. It can only consider the production of two products or types of products. As such, it is an example of an **economic model**. It is a simplification of reality in order to focus upon and understand certain key concepts.

The commonest example of the use of the production possibility frontier is for the production of consumer goods and services (those products that yield immediate satisfaction to consumers) and capital

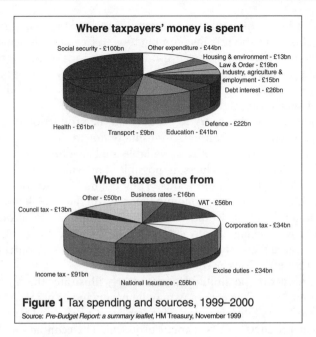

Figure 1 Tax spending and sources, 1999–2000

Source: *Pre-Budget Report: a summary leaflet*, HM Treasury, November 1999

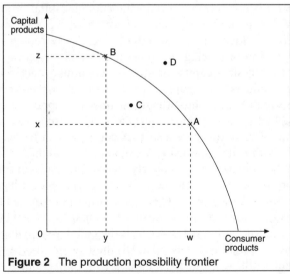

Figure 2 The production possibility frontier

goods and services (those products that are produced in order to produce more consumer products in the future) by an economy. Consumer products are put on one axis and **capital products** are placed on the other axis as shown in Figure 2.

The curved line represents the economy's production possibility frontier. It shows all the possible combinations of capital and consumer products that the economy can produce given the resources that are available to that economy. It is curved because less and less appropriate resources have to be used to make one type of product the more of that product that is demanded by society.

Economies will always try to produce on the production possibility frontier: it would be economic foolishness not to do so. By producing on the frontier, all resources available are being fully used in order to produce as many products as possible that will satisfy the greatest possible level of infinite wants. Thus points 'A' and 'B' could be production points for the economy. Point 'C' on the other hand would be undesirable as it would mean that not all of the economy's resources were being effectively put to use for productive purposes. More consumer wants could be met if the economy's resources were being more effectively used.

The production possibility frontier clearly illustrates the concept of opportunity cost. The economy may be producing at point 'A' on the production possibility frontier. This implies a production level of 'w' consumer products and 'x' capital products. The economy may then decide that it is not currently producing enough capital products and thus it wishes to increase production of these types of goods and services to 'z'. However, it can only do this by swapping resources currently used in producing consumer goods and services to the production of the desired capital products. This implies sacrificing some consumer products. In Figure 2, production of consumer products will have to fall to 'y'. Thus we can identify the opportunity cost of producing 'xz' more capital products as 'wy' consumer products.

It is helpful to notice here also that countries can be better off if they trade with other countries. A point such as point 'D' in Figure 2 cannot be achieved by a country producing and consuming all its own products. It would be desirable as it represents a higher level of production than any of the other points shown (and thus a higher level of satisfaction of consumer wants) but it is beyond the capabilities of the country. However, if the country **specialises** in producing those things that it is relatively best at producing and then **trades** some of those products with another country that is relatively better at producing different products, then it could find that point 'D' does become a possible consumption point. This suggests that international trade is economically desirable.

The key questions facing all economies

Given the fundamental economic problem that all economies have to face of how best to use their scarce resources to meet infinite human wants, there are really three key questions that then have to be answered:

1. What to produce? Given that not everything that is wanted can be produced, societies must decide which of the many wanted products should actually be produced.
2. How to produce? Once it is decided what is to be produced, it must be decided how to produce it. What techniques of production should be used to make the chosen products?
3. For whom to produce? Once the chosen production has occurred using the chosen production techniques, then decisions have to be made about who should receive the benefits of that production. What criteria should be used to decide who gets what?

Only when all these three questions have been answered will economies have 'answered' the fundamental problem of how scarce resources should best be used.

There are three types of ways that societies can organise themselves in order to try to answer these key questions:

1. **Planned (or command) economy.** An economy can allow its government to answer all of the key questions. The government decides upon everything that is produced, how it is produced and who then receives that production.
2. **Market (or capitalist) economy.** An alternative is that an economy allows the free market to answer the three questions. The free forces of supply and demand will dictate the products made as consumers seek to maximise their satisfaction through purchasing the goods and services that they most desire while producers seek profits by producing and selling the products that are demanded. Producers seeking profit will use production techniques that cost them least and then the distribution of the products will be dictated by the distribution of spending power in society.
3. **Mixed economy.** Societies might finally decide that they wish to organise the running of their economies somewhere between the two extremes of options one and two and use some mixture of the government and the market to answer the questions. The difficult issue then becomes to decide what is the appropriate mix between the government and the market.

It is clearly a crucial issue for economies as to whether governments or markets are likely to organise the best possible use of scarce resources. That is the key theme of much of the rest of this book.

KEY WORDS

Economics	Economic model
Scarce resources	Consumer products
Infinite wants	Capital products
Factors of production	Specialisation and trade
Choice	Planned or command economy
Allocation of resources	Market or capitalist economy
Opportunity cost	Mixed economy
Production possibility frontier	

Further reading

Anderton, A., Chapters 1 and 2 in *Economics*, 2nd edn, Causeway Press, 1995.

Maunder, P. *et al.*, Chapters 1 and 2 in *Economics Explained*, 3rd edn, Collins, 1995.

Grant, S., Chapters 1, 2 and 3 in George Stanlake's *Introductory Economics*, 7th edn, Longman, 2000.

Lipsey, R. and Chrystal, K., Chapter 1 in *Principles of Economics*, 9th edn, Oxford University Press, 1999.

Essay topics

1. Explain how the concept of opportunity cost is illustrated by a production possibility frontier.   [10 marks]
   [OCR, November, 1999]
2. (a) With the aid of a diagram, explain what is meant by a production possibility curve.   [10 marks]
   (b) Discuss the extent to which this concept can be used to explain why nations trade with each other.   [15 marks]
   [OCR, March, 1997]

Data response question

Demand for health care continues to increase. As people live longer they need more health care and as people get richer they demand better, more expensive health care. In addition improvements in technology continue to increase the range of treatments which are possible including ones which involve expensive operations and after care treatment. This has led successive governments to increase the resources available for the provision of health care. Figure A illustrates some resources being switched from, for example, education and defence to health care.

However, demand continues to outstrip supply. As a result the National Health Service (NHS) has to decide what treatments to offer. A decision by a hospital, for example, to increase the number of hip replacement operations may mean that it has to reduce the number of varicose vein operations it undertakes or even to stop infertility treatment altogether.

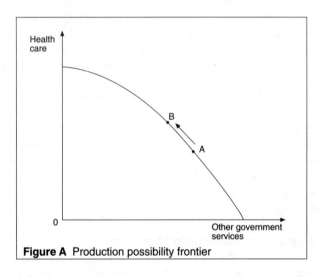

Figure A Production possibility frontier

1. Explain why demand for health care is increasing. [4 marks]
2. How does the market for health care illustrate the concept of scarcity? [4 marks]
3. Explain why the production possibility curve in Figure A is a curve and not a straight line. [6 marks]
4. Explain, using a production possibility diagram, the effect of more resources being made available for both health care and other government services. [6 marks]
5. Discuss the possible opportunity cost of more plastic surgery being undertaken by the NHS. [5 marks]

Chapter Two

Economic efficiency

'He who works his land will have abundant food, but he who chases fantasies lacks judgment.'
Proverbs, Chapter 12, Verse 11

The centrality of efficiency in economics

In chapter 1, we established that the essence of the subject of economics is a study of how we try best to use our scarce resources to meet our infinite wants. This suggests that being able to make a judgement about when resources are, or are not, being used in this 'best' possible way is very important. This is what '**economic efficiency**' is about.

In economics, *efficiency is a situation where all available scarce resources are being used in the most effective way possible to meet the greatest possible level of consumer wants.* There can be no uncertainty about the desirability of economic efficiency. Every type of economy, whether command, free market or somewhere in between must, according to the starting point of the subject of economics, aspire to achieve economic efficiency. We all want our resources to be used in the best possible way.

The two parts of economic efficiency

In order to be sure that we can state that economic resources are being used in the best possible way and thus that economic efficiency exists, two things must be true:

- Everything that is produced must be done so using the least possible amount of scarce resources. The lowest possible resource cost must be involved with every aspect of production. This is called **productive efficiency**.
- The right amount of the right products must be produced. Those products that yield most consumer satisfaction per unit of resource required to produce them should be the products produced. This is called **allocative efficiency**.

Only when both these parts of efficiency are present can economic efficiency be deemed to exist.

Productive efficiency

If resources are scarce, then it clearly makes sense to use the minimum amount of them possible when producing. If there are two possible ways of producing a particular good, method A and method B, and method A requires less resources than method B, then method A would lead to productive efficiency. On the other hand, method B would imply **inefficiency**. Resources are effectively being wasted.

A further way of understanding the concept of productive efficiency is by considering the cost schedules faced by any firm. This is shown in Figure 3.

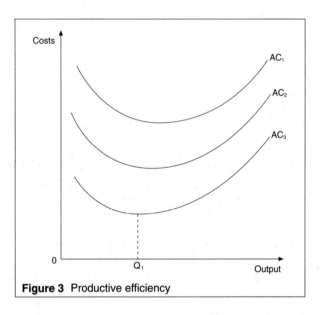

Figure 3 Productive efficiency

There are three possible average **cost curves** curves that the firm in Figure 3 could operate on, depending upon the method of production that is employed, AC_1, AC_2 or AC_3. If production is to be deemed efficient, then the firm must operate on the lowest possible cost curve that implies the lowest possible amount of resources are being used in production. In Figure 3, this means that the firm must produce on AC_3. *Productive efficiency means that firms will produce on their lowest cost curve.* Attempts by firms to produce the same products at a lower cost, such as the newspaper report about Barclay's on page 12, can be seen as efforts to move to a lower cost curve and a greater level of productive efficiency.

A further aspect of productive efficiency can also be seen from

Figure 3. Not only should the firm shown be producing on its lowest average cost curve, it should also be producing at the lowest point on that lowest cost curve. This point is indicated as output Q_1. When this occurs, **technical efficiency** is said to exist. Production is incurring the lowest level of unit costs possible.

Allocative efficiency

It is not enough simply to produce goods and services at the lowest possible resource cost. To have economic efficiency, the right products must be produced. Certain products may have been produced at the very lowest cost imaginable, but if they are goods and services that are not wanted as much as others that were not produced, then clearly resources have not been used in the best way possible. Thus, allocative efficiency is required as well as productive efficiency for economic efficiency to be deemed to exist. Firms can be seen to make moves towards allocative efficiency when they change production so that it is more in line with consumer preferences. The changes in banking services, as suggested in the article about Barclays Bank, represent such moves.

Barclays to cut 500 jobs and 200 more branches

PHILIP THORNTON

Up to 500 high street banking jobs will be axed as part of plans by Barclays Bank to close 200 branches next year, more than doubling the number of branches it has shut in the last nine years, and saving nearly £10m in annual costs. No decision has been taken on the exact number or location.

A spokesman said the bank had been reshaping its operations to put greater focus on new outlets such as Internet banking, and increasing the number of ATMs, better known as 'hole-in-the-wall' cash machines. There are more than 25,000 cash machines in Britain and the rise of automated banking in any form and the shift of bank-office processing to dedicated centres mean costly branches are not needed.

Customer research has shown the number of customers using branches regularly has fallen from more than a half to almost a third in recent years. Branch costs are still high.

Salomon Smith Barrey estimates the average costs of a transaction in a branch is 67.5p. For telephone banking it is 37p and the Internet costs just 7.5p.

The Independent, 15 November 1999

Allocative efficiency can be more technically defined than simply producing the right amount of the right goods and services. Specifically, allocative efficiency will exist when **price** equals **marginal cost**. Marginal cost represents the cost of producing the last unit of production. If this condition is true for all production throughout the whole of the economy, then resources will be devoted to precisely the right production to ensure the maximum amount of consumer wants are satisfied, given the resources that are available.

When the marginal cost of production is equal to the selling price, the price of products will reflect the true resource cost of production. When consumers make a decision to purchase a product, they will pay a price that reflects the level of satisfaction (or **utility**) that they derive from consuming that product. Thus, if a particular service gives a consumer £5 worth of satisfaction, the consumer is willing to pay up to £5 for that product. If that price of £5 also reflects the true resource cost of producing the service, then there is a matching of the use of the resource to the satisfaction that is derived from the service by the consumer. This is not true if marginal cost does not equal price:

- If price (say at £7) is greater than marginal cost (that is £5), then the service will be demanded but not as much as would be justified. In this case, not enough of the product is produced.
- If price (say at £3) is less than marginal cost (that is £5), then people will demand the service (and thus it will be produced) if it gives them just £3 worth of satisfaction. This represents a bad use of resources as the true cost of delivering £3 worth of satisfaction is £5 worth of resources. There is too much of the product produced in this case.

Pareto efficiency

A further way of defining the notion of efficiency in Economics was derived by the Italian economist Wilfredo Pareto. **Pareto efficiency** *exists when it is not possible to make any person better off without making someone else worse off.*

If a person can be made better off without any other person having to lose out, then resources cannot currently be deemed to be being used in the best possible way. More consumer wants can be satisfied by making better use of the resources that are available. This cannot be said when the only possible way of making any person better off is by making at least one person worse off. Such a reallocation of resources cannot be said with any certainty to have increased the satisfaction of consumer wants. This is because one person's gain in satisfaction cannot be meaningfully compared with another person's loss of satisfaction given the wholly subjective nature of such comparisons. Thus, once resources are allocated in the way stipulated by Pareto efficiency, we have to say that there is no obvious alternative means of allocation that will unambiguously raise the satisfaction of wants with the same resources.

Two economists, J. R. Hicks and N. Kaldor, suggested a possible way round this problem of not being able to compare the loss of satisfaction or benefit suffered by one person with the gain or benefit received by another. Their idea is known as the **compensation principle**. If the gainer can fully compensate the loser and still have some benefit left over, then overall there has been a net benefit through the transaction and it could be deemed to be desirable on economic grounds. This could allow the possibility of gains in economic welfare to be made even if one party initially loses through a trade.

Economic efficiency and the production possibility frontier

The production possibility frontier can helpfully be used to illustrate the different aspects of economic efficiency considered in this chapter. Referring back to Figure 1 (see page 6), the key point is that production must be occurring at a point (such as 'A' or 'B') somewhere on the production possibility frontier for economic efficiency to exist.

At point 'A' or 'B' there is productive efficiency. All resources are being fully used and there is no wasting of scarce resources. The production techniques that use the least possible resources are being employed. The economy in producing the maximum amount possible with the resources that are available to it. This is not true of point 'C'. Here, more could be produced with the economy's scarce resources and thus there is inefficiency.

At point 'A' or 'B' there is Pareto efficiency. The only way that one person could be made better off from one of these production positions is by making someone else worse off. Resources would have to be taken from one person and given to another. This is not true of point 'C'. Here, it is possible to increase production (of both capital and consumer products) without having to make any sacrifices. At least one person can be made better off without making anyone else worse off.

Allocative efficiency cannot be clearly indicated through the pro-

---

```
                        KEY WORDS

Economic efficiency         Price
Productive efficiency       Marginal cost
Allocative efficiency       Utility
Inefficiency                Pareto efficiency
Cost curves                 Compensation principle
Technical efficiency
```

duction possibility frontier. Whilst we may want the maximum amount of goods and services possible to be produced with our scarce resources, allocative efficiency requires that the right amount of the right product is produced. This can only be known by reference to the preferences of consumers. This information is not given by the production possibility frontier. Thus, we know that both points 'A' and 'B' yield productive efficiency but we cannot tell which one is closest to a position of allocative efficiency.

Further reading
Anderton, A., Chapter 34 in *Economics,* 2nd edn, Causeway Press, 1995.
Lipsey, R. and Chrystal, A., Chapter 18 in *Principles of Economics,* 9th edn, Oxford University Press, 1999.
Parkin, M. *et al.,* Chapters 3 and 6 in *Economics*, 4th edn, Addison Wesley, 2000.
Sloman, J., Chapter 1 in *Economics*, 4th edn, Prentice Hall, 2000.

Useful website
The Economist: www.economist.co.uk/

Essay topics
1. (a) Explain why it is important for an economy to produce a level of output located on its production possibility curve. [10 marks]
   (b) Discuss how it is possible for an economy to attain a point outside its current production possibility curve.   [15 marks]
   [OCR, November 1998]
2. (a) Explain what is meant by 'economic efficiency'.   [10 marks]
   (b) Discuss the benefits to consumers of achieving economic efficiency.   [15 marks]

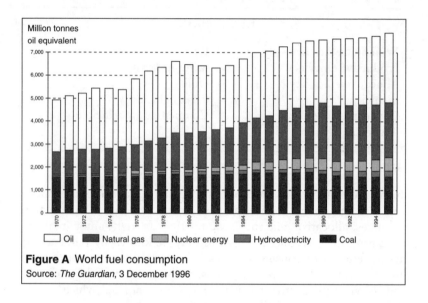

Figure A World fuel consumption
Source: *The Guardian*, 3 December 1996

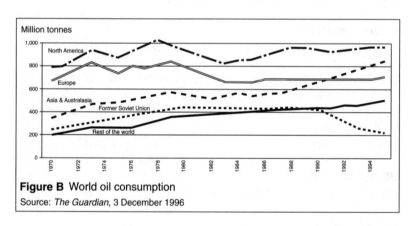

Figure B World oil consumption
Source: *The Guardian*, 3 December 1996

Data response question

This task is based on a question set by the Edexcel exam board in 1999. Study the material above concerning world fuel consumption and the costs of transport, and then answer the questions that follow.

Table A Environmental costs of transport (as estimated by the European Union)

	£ bn
Cars & motorcycles	153.1
Buses/freight	53.5
Rail*	3.8
iation*	13.2
Ships	0.6

* Passenger and freight

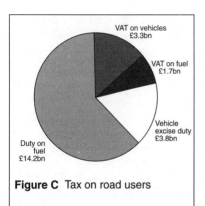

Figure C Tax on road users

Source: *The Financial Mail on Sunday*, 17 March 1996

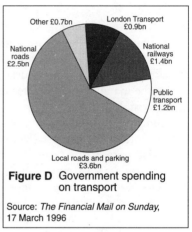

Figure D Government spending on transport

Source: *The Financial Mail on Sunday*, 17 March 1996

1. With reference to Figure A, suggest *two* factors which could account for the changing pattern of world fuel consumption since 1970. [4 marks]
2. With reference to Figure B, identify the trend in oil consumption in (i) Asia and Australasia and (ii) the former Soviet Union since 1990. How might these contrasting trends be explained? [5 marks]
3. With reference to Table A, how might the external costs of transport be estimated? [4 marks]
4. With reference to Figure C, contrast the effects of vehicle excise duty and duty on fuel on the use of different forms of transport. [6 marks]
5. Examine *two* policies, other than the use of the taxes shown in Figure C, which aim to reduce the costs of transport to the environment. [6 marks]

Chapter Three

Competition and efficiency

'*With free trade you can have both large-scale economic efficiency and small-scale political decentralisation.*'
Margaret Thatcher (1991)

The appeal of competition

It has long been argued by many economists that competition is a highly desirable economic state of affairs. Adam Smith in his *Wealth of Nations* (1776) famously argued the case in what is commonly regarded as the first economic textbook. The result of competitive forces is to produce a highly desirable state of affairs, something that cannot be matched by any alternative form of organising economies. The '**invisible hand**' of competition not only ensures that resources are allocated, but it also ensures that they are allocated well. The fundamental economic problem is solved as well as is possible within the constraints of the resources that are available.

A clearer way of expressing this argument in favour of the free market (and free market economies) is to say that *free markets lead to economic efficiency*. The '**laissez-faire**' approach of leaving everything to the forces of the free market achieves the most desirable outcome possible for an economy: efficiency. If this is so, then this is clearly a vital, in fact unanswerable in purely economic terms, case in favour of free markets and capitalist economies. The purpose of this chapter is to explain that case.

The nature of competition in economics

It is important to clarify what we mean by the term 'competition' in economics. There are various ways of trying to do this, but the clearest is to consider the oldest and best-known of all the descriptions of competition: **perfect competition**.

Perfect competition is another example of an economic model: a simplification of reality that uses assumptions to help to examine and analyse economic situations. It describes a state of affairs that represents the highest possible state of competition that could ever exist in an industry or a market. Such a state of affairs is said to exist if the following conditions apply:

- There are a large numbers of buyers and sellers in the market. This means that no individual producer or consumer can affect the market price or any other part of the market's operations.
- All products in the market are **homogeneous** (or identical). This implies that buyers will be totally indifferent and unconcerned as to which firm they purchase the product from.
- There is **perfect knowledge** in the market among both consumers and producers in the market.
- All firms in the industry produce the product with a common technology. Firms have identical cost schedules.
- All factors of production are perfectly **mobile**. Factors can be quickly and easily swapped between alternative forms of production.
- There are no **barriers to entry** into or exit from the industry for producers.
- All firms are **'price-takers'**. There will be just one price for all products sold in the market and firms can sell as much as they want at that market-determined price.

Any market or industry that conforms to all of these characteristics can be deemed to be in the fullest possible state of competition. Competition is 'perfect'. All firms in such an industry will find that, in the long run, they produce at a point illustrated in Figure 4.

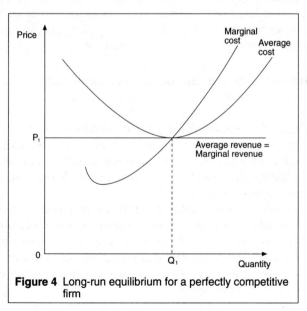

Figure 4 Long-run equilibrium for a perfectly competitive firm

19

The **average revenue** schedule is shown as horizontal for the firm. This is because the average revenue schedule is the same thing as the selling price of the product. It is known that this firm is a 'price-taker': it must simply accept the going market price and sell its products at that price. Thus, there is no variation in price (or average revenue) as the firm sells more or less products. When average revenue is constant like this, it is also bound to be equal to **marginal revenue** (as extra sales always yield the same amount of extra revenue with a constant selling price). Thus, marginal revenue is shown as identical to average revenue.

If the firm seeks to make maximum profit (as is assumed), then it will produce where marginal cost is equal to marginal revenue (the point of **profit maximisation**). This is indicated by output and sales level Q_1 in Figure 4. At this point, the firm is also breaking even: it is not earning either supernormal profit or making a loss. This is clear as **average cost** is equal to average revenue. This must be true in the long run in perfect competition:

- If there is **supernormal profit** being earned (average revenue is greater than average cost), then new firms will enter the market (there are no barriers to entry to prevent this from happening). This increase in supply will reduce price (and average revenue) until the supernormal profit has gone.
- If there is a loss (average revenue is less than average cost), then some firms will leave the market. This fall in supply will cause price (and average revenue) to rise until the loss has disappeared.

Free markets and the allocation of resources

The fundamental issue within economics is to secure the allocation of scarce resources between competing possible uses. The suggestion of **supply and demand** analysis is that free markets achieve this end without any person or organisation (such as a government) having to organise anything. The freely functioning forces of supply and demand allocate every single scarce resource in an effective fashion.

A simple supply and demand diagram, such as the one illustrated in Figure 5, shows how resources are allocated.

As every student of Economics knows, a freely working market will lead to an **equilibrium price** where supply is equal to demand. There is no instruction required from the government to make this happen, no careful gathering of information and organisation to ensure it is the case: it just happens. Producers, who seek profits, and consumers, who seek satisfaction (or utility) from consumption, will follow their

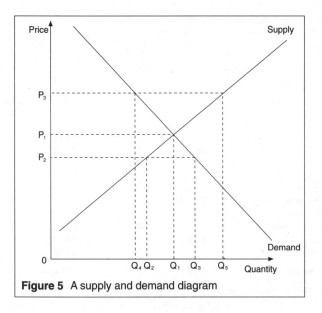

Figure 5 A supply and demand diagram

own interests and the market will adjust to deliver the equilibrium price of P_1 illustrated. This is associated with a level of production and sales of Q_1 of this product. The important point to note is that this represents an effective allocation of resources to the production and consumption of this product: there are neither too few nor too many resources devoted to this market. This can be seen by what would happen if a different price were established in the market:

- If price were at P_2, then there would be a greater demand for the product but producers would wish to produce and sell less. The result is that there would be a **shortage** of the product equal to Q_2Q_3. Too few resources would be devoted to this product.
- If price were at P_3, then there would be less demand for the product but producers would wish to produce and sell more. This would result in a **surplus** of the product equal to Q_4Q_5. Too many resources would be devoted to the making of the product.

The effectiveness of the price system in a free market can be taken a stage further when thinking about what happens if consumer preferences change over time. For example, suppose that a particular product becomes more popular over time as average **real incomes** rise. A good example of this would be from the figures in Table 1 from the Office for National Statistics that show the great growth in the demand for leisure services over the past thirty years in the U.K. Such

Table 1 UK average household weekly spending

| | 1998–99 | | 1968 | |
	£ per week	% of total expenditure	£ per week (1998–99 prices)	% of total expenditure
Leisure	£59.80	17	£21.13	9
Food & non-alcoholic drinks	£58.90	17	£63.90	26
Housing	£57.20	16	£30.74	13
Motoring	£51.70	15	£25.41	10
Household goods & services	£48.60	14	£28.81	12
Clothing & footwear	£21.70	6	£21.54	9
Alcoholic drink	£14.00	4	£9.92	4
Personal goods & services	£13.30	4	£6.21	3
Fuel & power	£11.70	3	£15.01	13
Fares & other travel costs	£8.30	2	£6.35	3
Tobacco	£5.80	2	£12.59	5
Miscellaneous	£1.20	0	£0.73	0
Total expenditure	**£352.20**		**£242.34**	

Source: *Social Trends*, Office of National Statistics, November 1999

an increase in demand could be illustrated on a supply and demand diagram as in Figure 6.

The rise in demand for leisure services is shown by the movement in the demand schedule from D_1 to D_2. The desired outcome of this is that more resources should be devoted to the production of such services. This is allocative efficiency: ensuring that the right amount of the right products is produced. The forces of supply and demand ensure that this happens:

1. The higher demand pushes up the price of the product as illustrated in Figure 6 by the move in equilibrium price from P_1 to P_2. With the higher price, producers wish to increase production in order to make the most of the new profit opportunity. Thus production and sales rise from Q_1 to Q_2. More resources are allocated to the production of leisure services.

2. The labour market moves to provide the necessary workforce for the higher production of leisure services. The higher demand for leisure leads to a higher demand for workers in this sector of the labour market. This causes the **equilibrium wage** to rise (as equilibrium price rises in Figure 6). Workers are thus attracted into this occupation and so the necessary workforce is provided to produce the higher level of leisure services. The same process is true for the markets for other factors of production.

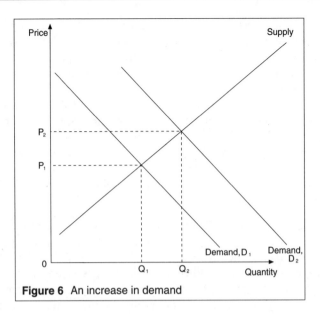

Figure 6 An increase in demand

3. In the long run, the long-run supply schedule could also move to the right as more resources are devoted to producing something such as leisure services and costs fall due to economies of scale. This leads to greater productive efficiency and benefits the consumer through lower prices.

The opposite forces could be at work with a product that lost its popularity with consumers (such as tobacco according to the Office for National Statistics). The forces of supply and demand would ensure that resources were moved away from the production of such products.

What we have been describing is what Adam Smith in his *Wealth of Nations* termed the 'invisible hand'. Unseen and unorganised, the free forces of supply and demand have worked in the economy in order to guide scarce resources into the appropriate line of production so as to ensure that the greatest possible level of consumer wants are satisfied.

Free markets and productive efficiency

It can clearly be reasoned that competition can lead to productive efficiency. This can be understood through the 'carrot and stick' of competition and its effects upon the behaviour of firms:

1. The carrot of competition. The carrot of the free market can be seen as the incentive given by the possibility of earning profit. This incentive will drive firms to seek the lowest possible cost techniques of production. Profit can only be maximised if costs are at their lowest possible level.
2. The stick of competition. If the incentive of profits is not enough to drive firms to minimise their costs, then the threat of bankruptcy will be. A firm in a competitive market will have no choice but to produce at the lowest possible cost because its competitors will do so. A failure to achieve **cost minimisation** will mean an inability to compete with those firms who have minimised their costs.

Thus, firms in free competitive markets will produce on their lowest possible cost curve. Further, where there is perfect competition, then technical efficiency will also be present. This is clear from Figure 4. Here, the long-run equilibrium of the firm is given as the output level Q_1. The conditions of a perfectly competitive market imply that this will always be at the lowest point on the firm's average cost curve, the point of technical efficiency.

Free markets and allocative efficiency

In the same way as with productive efficiency, it can equally be asserted that the 'carrot and stick' of free, competitive markets will lead to allocative efficiency:

1. The carrot of competition. The desire to make profit will ensure that firms produce those products that consumers most want to purchase. Only by doing this can significant revenue, and hence profits, be earned.
2. The stick of competition. There is the threat of bankruptcy if firms fail to produce those products that consumers will demand the most as other firms in a competitive market will succeed in producing such products. Custom will be lost and the firm may not survive.

The free market thus leads to a situation where consumers dictate what is produced. This is referred to in economics as '**consumer sovereignty**'. The consumer reigns and whatever he or she most wants is what firms are obliged to produce. Such a situation has been likened to an '**economic democracy**':

- The candidates in this democracy are the products.
- The votes are money.

- The polling booths are markets.
- The voters are consumers.

Consumers enter markets and cast their votes (in the form of money) for the products that they wish to purchase. The greater the number of votes cast, the greater the number of products produced (similar to candidates being elected). This is a situation of consumer sovereignty and allocative efficiency.

The characteristics of perfect competition can also be seen as leading to the specific requirement of allocative efficiency, price equalling marginal cost $(P = MC)$. Referring once more to Figure 4, the equilibrium point of Q_1 is a point at which price (or average revenue) is equal to marginal cost. This will always be true under perfect competition. If this is replicated throughout the economy, then precisely the right amount of resources will be allocated to the appropriate forms of production.

Free markets and Pareto efficiency

The economist Milton Friedman once stated:

> 'The key insight of Adam Smith's Wealth of Nations is misleadingly simple: if an exchange between two parties is voluntary, it will not take place unless both believe that they will benefit from it. Most economic fallacies derive from the neglect of this simple insight, from the tendency to assume that there is a fixed pie, that only one party can gain at the expense of another.'

Friedman can be paraphrased as stating here that free markets will lead to Pareto efficiency. If all trade is free and unhindered in competitive markets, then it will always take place as long as both the producer and the consumer feel that they benefit from the trade. The moment that either one of them does not see the benefit in the trade, then it will not take place. No one can force either a producer or a consumer into a trade that makes him or her worse off. The implication of this is that free trade must lead to Pareto efficiency. Trading will take place as long as it makes everyone better off. Trading will not take place if the only way to make one person better off is to make someone else worse off.

Conclusion

The clear conclusion of all the points made in this chapter is that free, competitive markets will lead to economic efficiency in all of its different forms. The implication is clear: the best way to run an economy is to leave it all to the market: 'laissez-faire' will achieve the optimum allocation of resources. Governments should not interfere. It is the sort of view expressed in the article from *The Economist*.

Business and competition

Competition is the best stimulus for innovation and efficiency, the chancellor proclaimed in his budget. He cited the work of Professor Steve Nickell of the London School of Economics, whose 1996 article 'Competition and Corporate Performance' demonstrated the link between competitive pressures and higher productivity. So why on earth did Mr Brown spoil the effect by clogging up his budget with complex tax incentives for small businesses, which mean they may spend less time innovating and more reshuffling their tax affairs?

Effective competition policy sets rules and then lets the market get on with it. Mr Brown, instead, seems determined to fiddle about with the market, chopping and changing the business tax regime to no obvious effect.

The Economist, 13 March 1999

KEY WORDS

Invisible hand	Average cost
Laissez-faire	Supernormal profit
Perfect competition	Supply and demand analysis
Homogeneous products	Equilibrium price
Perfect knowledge	Shortage
Mobile factors	Surplus
Barriers to entry	Real incomes
Price-takers	Equilibrium wage
Average revenue	Cost minimisation
Marginal revenue	Consumer sovereignty
Profit maximisation	Economic democracy

Further reading

Begg, D. *et al.*, Chapter 15 in *Economics*, 5th edn, McGraw Hill, 1997.

Lipsey, R. and Chrystal, K., Chapter 18 in *Principles of Economics*, 9th edn, Oxford University Press.

Sloman, J., Chapter 11 in *Economics*, 4th edn, Prentice Hall, 2000.

Healey, N. and Cook, M., Chapter 7 in *Supply Side Economics*, 3rd edn, Heinemann Educational, 1996.

Useful website

Biz/ed: www.bized.ac.uk

Essay topics

1. (a) Explain what is meant by 'perfect competition'. [10 marks]
   (b) Discuss whether free markets will achieve efficiency.
   [15 marks]
2. (a) Distinguish between productive and allocative efficiency.
   [10 marks]
   (b) Discuss whether an increase in competition in a market will achieve efficiency. [15 marks]

Data response question

This task is based on a question set by the Edexcel Examination Board in 1998. Study the two tables and the graph below, and then answer the questions that follow.

Table A GDP and health expenditure in selected countries

Country	GDP per capita $, 1990	Health expenditure, 1990				
		Total $m	Per head $	Total %	Public %	Private %
Spain	11,020	32,375	831	6.6	5.2	1.4
New Zealand	12,680	3,150	925	7.2	5.9	1.3
UK	16,100	59,623	1,039	6.1	5.2	0.9
USA	21,790	690,667	2,763	12.6	5.6	7.0
Norway	23,120	7,782	1,835	7.4	7.0	0.4
Switzerland	32,680	16,916	2,520	7.5	5.1	2.4

Source: *World Development Report,* Oxford University Press, 1992

Table B UK Expenditure on the National Health Service

Year	Government expenditure on NHS £m	Total general government expenditure £m	NHS expenditure as a % of total general government expenditure	NHS expenditure as a % of GDP
1984/85	16,312	134,464	12.1	5.8
1985/86	17,434	147,059	11.8	5.7
1986/87	18,982	153,833	12.3	5.8
1987/88	20,881	166,466	12.5	5.8
1988/89	23,080	183,471	12.6	5.7
1989/90	25,029	198,401	12.6	5.7
1990/91	27,911	213,343	13.1	5.8
1991/92	31,841	219,425	14.5	6.4
1992/93	35,353	220,872	16.0	6.8
1993/94	37,355	225,738	16.6	6.8

Source: *Annual Abstract of Statistics*, HMSO, 1995

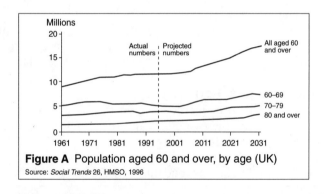

Figure A Population aged 60 and over, by age (UK)
Source: *Social Trends* 26, HMSO, 1996

1. Examine reasons for the state provision of health care in developed nations such as those in Table A. [6 marks]
2. With reference to Table B and Figure A, discuss *three* possible reasons for the change in the UK's spending on the National Health Service between 1984 and 1994. [9 marks]
3. With reference to Table A, examine *one* reason for the differences in private sector health expenditure between the countries shown. [4 marks]
4. In September 1995 an organisation called Healthcare 2000 stated that '*if funding levels in the state-owned National Health Service remain the same in real terms the gap between resources and demand will increase further*'. Examine the meaning and implications of the phrase printed in italics. [6 marks]

Chapter Four

Market failures

'*People of the same trade seldom meet together but the conversation ends in a conspiracy against the public, or in some diversion to raise prices.*'
Adam Smith

Problems with the market

The suggestion of chapter 3 was that the free market was the best possible way to deliver economic efficiency in an economy. If everything were left alone, resources would be allocated so as to satisfy the greatest possible level of consumer wants. The suggestion of this chapter is that this is not the case. There are reasons why free markets may well not deliver the best possible allocation of scarce resources.

When free markets do not deliver optimum resource allocation they are said to 'fail'. **Market failure** exists *when free markets fail to deliver economic efficiency.* This chapter examines the possible reasons for any such failure. It concentrates on the following four key areas:

1. The existence of externalities.
2. Public goods.
3. The problems of information failure.
4. The breakdown of perfect competition.

This chapter considers each of these factors in turn and discusses how they mean that free markets will lead to inefficiency in their presence.

Externalities

An **externality** *exists when a* **third party** *is affected by the actions of others.* If a person or group of people not directly involved in a decision made by other people is affected by that decision, then there is an externality. I did not make the decision to drop litter in the street, but the decision of others to do so affects my level of enjoyment in walking down the street. I did not have anything to do with the Christmas lights put up in a nearby town, but I can enjoy seeing them. All these are externalities: as a third party, I had no role in making the decisions mentioned. However, I was affected by these decisions. My level of satisfaction with life was either adversely or positively affected by the actions of others with whom I had no negotiation.

Similarly, I may take decisions that have an impact upon third parties that were not involved in the decision-making process. For example, the decision I take to go on holiday overseas could have an impact upon a range of other people, thus creating externalities. This is suggested in the article about ethical tourism that suggests a number of ways in which holiday-makers could have a negative impact upon others. All these negative impacts are examples of externalities.

The existence of externalities causes markets to fail. The essence of the problem is that the third party is not involved in the economic decision-making process. Thus, the impact of the decision (that will affect the allocation of scarce resources) upon the third party is not taken into account. However, it should be: that impact has a real effect upon the level of satisfaction (or utility) of the third party and needs to be taken into account in determining if scarce resources should be allocated in the way selected by those involved in the decision-making

Sun, sea and a little ethnic cleansing: dilemmas of the moral traveller

JEREMY ATIYAH

Ethical considerations may never play a serious role in your choice of holiday destination, but even if they do, it is not easy to judge what makes a destination 'safe'.

A major difficulty, for example, is the issue of how well the employees in the local tourist industry are being treated. Are they paid fairly? Do they have tolerable working conditions? Or are they treated as something close to slave labour?

There's also money. Is the cash you spend going into the pockets of local people, or the pockets of tour operators back home? And are there opportunities for locals and tourists to relate to each other on any remotely equal basis?

Then you need to think about the consequences of tourism for the environment. In places such as Goa, tourism stands accused of using all the clean water for the needs of luxury hotels. In Spain it goes to keeping golf courses green.

The only simple way to ensure that your tourist dollars do enter the local economy is to spend your money at locally owned and managed concerns.

And if you are still worried, the answer is probably not to go away at all. For your aeroplane will almost certainly cause more pollution than anything else you do during your holiday.

The Independent on Sunday, 14 November 1999

process. The result is that resources may end up not being allocated in the best possible way: there may not be economic efficiency.

Specifically, it is possible to identify both negative and positive externalities. Both of them will lead to economic inefficiency.

Negative externalities

A **negative externality** *exists when the* **social cost** *of an activity is greater than the* **private cost**. To put it another way, there are costs imposed upon a third party that are in addition to the costs involved to those who make the decision to carry out an activity.

- A private cost is the cost of an activity incurred by those directly involved in the activity itself. For example, a firm producing a chemical product incurs the costs of the raw materials required and the labour necessary to make the product.
- The social cost of an activity is the cost incurred by the whole of society due to a particular activity. This will always include all private costs, but it could include some further costs in addition to private costs. In the example of the company making chemical products, these might be any pollution generated in the production that led to clean-up costs being imposed on others and the road congestion created near the company that increases delivery times for other companies.

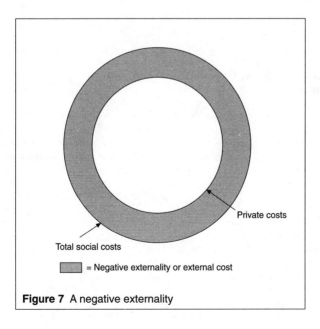

Private costs

Total social costs

▨ = Negative externality or external cost

Figure 7 A negative externality

It is possible that private costs represent all the social costs of an activity. In this case, there is no externality as private costs = social costs. However, when social costs exceed private costs, then an **external cost** or negative externality is said to exist. This can be illustrated as in Figure 7. Private costs are shown as a subset of total social costs. They are part, but not all, of social costs. The difference between the social cost and the private cost, as shown by the shaded area, represents the external cost or negative externality.

The problem with negative externalities is that they lead to **over-production**. The market decision only takes account of the private costs of an economic decision as these are the only costs directly borne by the decision-maker(s). No account is taken of the wider external costs that do not have to be borne by the decision-maker(s). The result is that too many scarce resources are used in the production of the good or service that generates negative externalities. This is clearly seen in Figure 8. The free market is seen as delivering a level of output Q_1 and a price P_1. This is the point where marginal private cost (MPC) (the same as the supply schedule in a perfectly competitive market) is equal to average revenue (AR) (or demand). This standard equilibrium of the free competitive market where supply is equal to demand does not, however, represent the optimum level of production. This is given

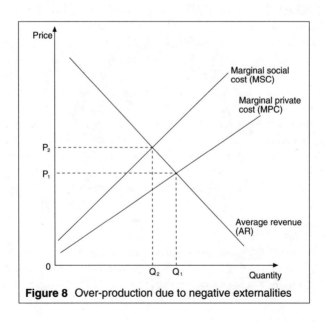

Figure 8 Over-production due to negative externalities

by the output Q_2 and the associated price of P_2. This is the point yielded by the intersection of the marginal social cost (MSC) schedule with the average revenue schedule. Marginal social costs are greater than marginal private costs due to the existence of external costs or negative externalities. This means that the marginal social cost schedule is to the left of the private marginal cost schedule and thus that the quantity that is given by the intersection of MSC with AR is less than the quantity given by the intersection of MPC with AR. The free market has led to an over-production of the product equal to Q_2Q_1. There has been a misallocation of resources by the free market.

Another way of understanding this problem of negative externalities is to recall the concept of allocative efficiency. The problem illustrated by Figure 8 is that the market price is less than marginal social cost. This leads to too much being produced and allocative inefficiency.

There are various significant examples of negative externalities. One is **road traffic congestion**. Road congestion can be seen as a negative externality associated with road travel. As with all negative externalities, the result is that too much of the product generating the externality (in this case road travel) is produced.

The decision to travel anywhere by car is taken by an individual on an individual assessment of the costs and benefits involved for that individual. The cost of the journey will be measured in terms of the fuel costs and time involved. The benefits will be seen as the value of arriving at the desired destination (and, occasionally, the pleasure of the travel). The problem with this decision is that it takes no account of the fact that there are other road users who may be affected by the decision. Specifically, this decision does not concern itself with the fact that by becoming another road user, further traffic congestion may be created. Such increased traffic congestion is clearly a social cost (the increased time and difficulty created in the journeys of all other road users) but it is not a private cost. It is an external cost. Thus, we see the market fail: the price of road travel is too cheap and there are too many scarce resources used in road travel.

Positive externalities

A **positive externality** *exists when the* **social benefit** *of an activity exceeds the* **private benefit**. To put it another way, there are benefits received by a third party from an activity that are in addition to the benefits received by the decision-makers.

- A private benefit of an activity is the benefit received by those directly involved in the activity. For example, the decision of a fine musician to practise is made on the basis of the benefit received by that musician in terms of improved personal competence at the piece of music and instrument played.
- The social benefit of an activity is the benefit to the whole of society received through an activity. These will include all private benefits but may include some further **external benefits**. For example, with the fine musician practising his or her musical piece, those people fortunate to listen at the time gain satisfaction (or utility) from the practice.

The problem with positive externalities is that they lead to **under-production**. The free market decision only takes account of the private benefits gained but fails to consider the further external benefits that are part of the total social benefit. Thus the activity is under-valued by the market and insufficient resources are devoted to its production. This situation can be seen in Figure 9. The free market outcome is represented by price P_1 and quantity Q_1. This represents the supply and demand equilibrium generated by the intersection of the marginal social cost schedule (MSC: there are assumed to be no negative externalities) and the private benefit (or demand) schedule (PB). The problem with this is that it has failed to take into account the full social benefits as represented by the schedule SB. This suggests that

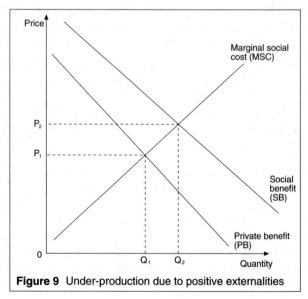

Figure 9 Under-production due to positive externalities

the socially desirable level of production would be Q_2 with an associated price of P_2. The free market has generated the wrong price and quantity due to the failure to take into account the full social benefits of the activity. There is thus an under-production equal to Q_1Q_2. Too few scarce resources are devoted to producing this product.

Once more, the problem can be understood in terms of allocative efficiency. The market price at Q_1 is below the 'true' value as represented by the social benefit schedule. Thus, the 'true' value is greater than marginal cost at Q_1. This means that there is an under-production and allocative inefficiency.

Education is often identified as a service with important positive externalities. The private decision made about whether to receive education (either for oneself or one's children) is based upon a calculation of the private benefits that are to be gained compared with the private costs that will be incurred. However, it seems reasonable to suggest that there are further social benefits in educating a person that go beyond the private benefits received. These might include the development of more responsible citizens, better workers, better poets and more interesting people to engage in conversation. The problem with market provision of education could thus be that there will be an under-provision as all such external benefits are not taken into account in the market decision.

Public goods

Public goods *are goods that possess the characteristics of* **non-excludability** *and* **non-rivalry**:

- Non-excludability means that once the good has been produced for the benefit of one person, it is impossible to stop others from benefiting from it.
- Non-rivalry means that as more people consume the good and enjoy its benefits, the benefits to those already consuming the good are not reduced.

It can be seen that public goods, as defined above, are the opposite of **private goods**. A private good, such as a chocolate bar, is excludable. I can stop others benefiting from it by eating it myself. It is also rival. If others take a bite from my chocolate bar, then there is less of it left for me to enjoy.

There are various examples of public goods that can be identified as possessing the two necessary attributes:

1. A lighthouse. Once a lighthouse has been built and operated for the benefit of one boat in a particular area of the sea, it is impossible for all others not to benefit in the same way. In addition, as more boats benefit from being warned away from some dangerous rocks, that does not reduce the benefits from those already receiving the warning.
2. A firework display. Once a large firework display is provided in an area for at least one person, it is hard to stop others also benefiting from this display. As more people watch, that will not obviously reduce the benefit to those already watching.
3. A national defence system. Once a decision has been made by a nation to attempt to protect at least one citizen from external attack by a potential foe then all citizens are likely to be equally protected. The benefit to any one citizen of such protection is not in any way diminished due to the protection received by others.

The problem associated with public goods is that they may not be produced at all in the free market. The incentives that are at work that are seen to drive economic behaviour in the free market lead to the logical possibility that a public good will not be produced even though people place a positive value upon it and would, in principle, be willing to pay for it. Thus, scarce resources should be devoted to the production of the public good but they are not. This represents a clear market failure.

The essence of the problem is that rational, utility-maximising individuals will attempt to '**free ride**'. No rational individual will be willing to pay for the production of a public good for his or her own use knowing that others can then benefit from its use without having to make any payment. The thing to do is to wait until someone else provides the public good and then enjoy its consumption without having to make any payment. In other words, people will try to gain a free ride. The problem with this is that if everyone behaves in this way then the product will never be provided.

There is still a problem if a producer attempts to organise an appropriate means of payment for the public good. It might be reasonable for the producer to ask consumers how much they would value the consumption of the public good if it were available. On the basis of this information, appropriate charges might then be made to each consumer and it could be profitable for the producer to produce the good. However, the problem of free riding remains. There is a clear incentive for consumers not to reveal their value for the public good in order not to have to pay. They know that they can benefit once it is provided and thus not revealing its worth means the consumption could be enjoyed free of charge. The result of this behaviour is that once more the good will not be produced.

Quasi-public goods

There is a further category of public goods known as **quasi-public goods**. *A quasi-public good is a good that possesses some but not all of the characteristics of a public good.* It is not a pure public good, but it is closer to being a public good than a private good.

A beach by the sea might be an example of a quasi-public good. It appears naturally to be non-excludable, although private owner-ship could allow the possibility of exclusion being introduced. However, it is the characteristic of non-rivalry that is most notable. Initially, this characteristic applies to a beach. As a few more people enjoy the beach, the enjoyment of those already there is not obvi-ously affected. However, there reaches a key point at which this is no longer true. After a certain point, any extra people attempting to enjoy the beach start to diminish the enjoyment of those who are already there. After a certain point, this problem can become chronic as crowding leads to a very serious reduction in the enjoyment of everyone using the beach.

This will be seen to be a significant factor in the understanding of environmental problems. In some ways, the essence of environmen-tal problems is that the environment is not a pure public good but a quasi-public good. However, there are other significant examples. Roads might be seen in this light. Up to a point, the principle of non-rivalry can be seen to apply. However, after a certain point, rivalry sets in. Any extra road-users lead to a reduction in benefit of those already using the road in terms both of safety and travel times. The resource becomes inappropriately used and there is a degree of mar-ket failure due to over-consumption.

The same problem can be seen with the increasing concern over the safety of air travel expressed in the article 'Crowded skies bring new safety warnings'. The sky appears to be a public good. It is non-excludible and seems non-rival. However, the article suggests that there is a certain point at which this ceases to be true. After a cer-tain point, the safety of all air travellers is affected by the addition of any more aeroplanes. This suggests that over-consumption may occur.

Crowded skies bring new safety warnings

PAUL MARSTON

Aircraft congestion over southern England has provoked an upsurge in confidential 'overload' warnings from air traffic controllers.

An internal Civil Aviation Authority bulletin records seven occasions last month when controllers deemed the volume of flights too great to guarantee safety. The bulletin is further evidence of what a committee of MPs recently described as the 'severe pressure' faced by staff at the London Area and Terminal Control Centre, which handles two-thirds of flights in United Kingdom airspace.

The centre, at West Drayton, near Heathrow, is forecast to manage 1.7 million flights this year, 25 per cent more than four years ago. Controllers say that attempts to 're-sectorise' airspace to create more capacity have led to increases in traffic in other sectors of nearly 30 per cent in the last year. A controller can sometimes handle up to 40 aircraft at once.

A senior pilot, who has seen the bulletin, said: 'The system is like a complicated road junction, which manages for years with steadily rising numbers of cars. You get a sudden jump in traffic, and things go wrong all over the place.'

The Daily Telegraph, 27 April 1998

Information failure

Where there is **imperfect information**, markets are likely to fail. There are a number of ways in which this can be seen to be the case, but three are particularly notable:

1. The case of **merit** and **de-merit goods**.
2. **Inappropriate trades** occurring due to information failures.
3. Problems with **insurance markets**.

Merit and de-merit goods

A merit good is a product that is better for a person than that person realises. The benefits to the consumer are in excess of the benefits that the consumer believes to exist for himself or herself. In other words, there is an information failure. Consumers are not in full possession of all the required information to be able to make the 'best' or 'right' decision about how much of a product to consume. They thus choose to consume too little of a merit good. Insufficient scarce resources are devoted to the production of merit goods and the market fails to deliver economic efficiency.

The problem created by a merit good can be understood by referring to Figure 10. This indicates a difference between the perceived benefit of consuming the product enjoyed by the consumer and the 'real' benefit.

The consumer believes that he or she will enjoy the level of benefit indicated by the average revenue (or demand) schedule AR_1. This leads to a market equilibrium of quantity Q_1 and price P_1. However, AR_1 is based on inaccurate information. The actual level of benefit that would be received by the consumer from consuming the product is indicated by the higher level of benefits suggested in AR_2. This would lead to a quantity of Q_2 of the product being consumed with a market price of P_2. Thus, the problem with the free market provision of merit goods is that there will be an under-production: too few scarce resources will be allocated to their production.

The problem with merit goods can be seen to be the same as the problem with products that have positive externalities associated with them: there is an under-production due to a failure of the market to register the true benefit of the product. However, the reasons for this differ between the two types of products. With a product generating positive externalities, it is the external benefit that is not registered. With a merit good, it is the value of the product to the consumer that is not fully appreciated. In practice, however, there may be little need to clarify this distinction as merit goods always tend to be products that also generate positive externalities.

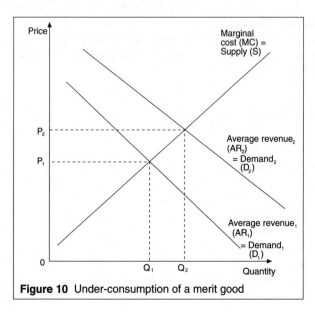

Figure 10 Under-consumption of a merit good

There are various possible examples of merit goods. Health care is often seen as a good example due to the lack of knowledge of potential consumers about the possible beneficial effects of such things as preventative health care. A seat-belt in a car could be seen in this sort of light. This is discussed more fully in chapter 9. Education is also often classified as a merit good. It is suggested that the potential recipients of education are not always fully aware of the potential benefits to themselves (both in terms of enhanced future earning power and a greater enjoyment of life in a more general sense) or the children for whom they may be making the decision. If this is so, then the free market may lead to an under-provision of education.

It is important to note that it is sometimes suggested that there is an element of 'paternalism' in the concept of merit goods. In other words, there are judgements implicitly being made about how good certain products are for people with the suggestion that some people make wrong judgements about what they should consume. This is a difficult area for economists as 'positive' economics claims to be free from value judgements. Judgements about merit goods may represent such value judgements.

A de-merit good is a product that is worse for a person than that person realises. It is the opposite of a merit good. People believe the product to have greater benefits for them than it actually has. Thus, in Figure 10, the benefits perceived are represented by the schedule AR_2. However, the 'true' lower benefits of consuming the product are represented by AR_1. The result of this misperception is that there is an over-production and over-consumption of the product. Too many scarce resources are devoted to its production and thus the market fails.

Products such as illegal drugs are often cited as possible examples of de-merit goods: the short-run enjoyment is considered by the consumer but the longer-run problems and dangers are either unknown or not properly considered. This is the message of the article about illegal drugs (opposite) that suggests there is a dangerous misperception amongst some people of their likely dangers. These drugs may thus be over-consumed due to an over-valuation of their benefits.

Inappropriate trades
Imperfect information is likely to lead to a lack of Pareto efficiency.

Chapter 3 suggested that the free market would lead to Pareto efficiency as trades would only take place as long as both parties knew that they would gain from a trade. Thus, free trade will lead to all mutually advantageous trades occurring and a position of Pareto

Heroin chic, ecstasy myth noted in US report

ELAINE MONAGHAN

Heroin chic, a pernicious belief that dance club drug ecstasy is safe, and growing cocaine use in Europe were insidious trends identified in the U.S. drugs report for 1999.

Gone is the image of a heroin addict dying in an alley with a dirty needle in his or her arm, replaced by glamorous notions of chic models sniffing purer forms, the State Department's report said. The drug is attracting more US teenagers, it added.

'For today's prospective heroin user in the United States, needles are not obligatory,' it said, explaining that top-grade Colombian heroin could be sniffed rather than injected.

'There have been prominent heroin addicts known to have preserved the façade of a normal life for decades, a fact that can feed youthful scepticism over heroin's real dangers,' it added.

Bony, pale-faced models with dark make-up smudged around their eyes had the 'heroin chic' image of the 1990s which critics said gave the drug a good name.

Photographer Davide Sorrenti, whose picture of his model girlfriend slumped on a bed with portraits of drug culture heroes drew condemnation from President Bill Clinton, later died of a drug overdose at the age of 20.

Designer drug ecstasy, which users say gives them a feeling of well-being and energy, is believed to be relatively safe. 'It is seen as a non-addictive stimulant,' the report said.

In the United States, slightly more than four per cent and five per cent of 10th and 12th graders in their mid- to late teens reported using the drug, it noted.

Designer drug producers can find recipes on the Internet and deadly batches spill onto club scenes globally.

For example, 'Flatliners' – named after the image on a heart monitor when a patient's heart stops beating – killed at least three people in Britain in 1998. Police said buyers of the drug thought they were getting ecstasy.

Reuters, 1 March 2000

efficiency. However, if there is imperfect information upon which people make their decisions to trade, then a person could agree to trade and later realise that he or she has been made worse off by doing so. The economy would thus have moved away from Pareto efficiency. Advertising could be seen as an important possible source of misinformation in modern market economies. The benefits of a product could be seen as being portrayed as greater than they really are.

Insurance markets

A market that may fail due to imperfect information is the market for insurance. There are two specific problems associated with free insurance markets:

1. **Adverse selection.**
2. **Moral hazard.**

The problem of adverse selection is likely to occur in insurance markets as insurers find it hard to gain sufficient information about their potential clients. Clients may well be aware of how great a risk they have of having to claim from the insurers at some point in the future. However, it may not be to their advantage to divulge this information to the insurer as it would be likely to have an adverse effect on the premium that they were charged. For example, with health care, it would be tempting for a person not to divulge to the health care insurance provider that he or she may have inherited a genetic disorder that would be likely to require considerable future health care.

The failure of the insurance provider to find out the differing levels of risk associated with different customers means that a similar price (or premium) may have to be charged to all or most customers. The problem with this is that it will represent very good value for high risk customers and very bad value for low risk customers. The likely outcome is that low risk customers cease to purchase the overpriced insurance cover and thus the provider is left with bad risks only. This is the problem of adverse selection. It can lead to partial or total failure of an insurance market as providers find that they cannot make a profit and many low risk customers do not insure themselves when they would like some insurance but only at an appropriately priced premium.

The problems of insurance markets are compounded by the further difficulty of moral hazard. This describes the possible effect on people's behaviour of being insured. There is a clear incentive for people to behave in a less careful fashion once insured. With household insurance, less security measures may be taken to prevent burglary than by the person who is not insured. This means that an accurate assessment of risks by an insurance provider leading to an appropriate premium may prove to be too generous a price once behaviour becomes less careful after the insurance has been taken out. This may lead to the provision of insurance becoming unprofitable and thus the market to fail.

It is interesting to note the sorts of steps that private insurers, such as in the car insurance market, take to try to overcome the problems of insurance markets outlined above:

- Proxies for individual risk are used. Whilst it may not be possible accurately to assess the risk of every individual there is information available that can help to give some information about likely risk. This is particularly true with the age of the customer and the type of car driven. Thus, premiums vary according to both of these factors.
- No claims' discounts do much to reduce the problem of moral hazard. They create an incentive to behave carefully and not to claim, unlike systems where there is no penalty for a claim.

Lack of perfect competition

The benefits of competition and the free market discussed in chapter 3 rested on the assumption that the free markets were perfectly competitive. As soon as free markets are not perfectly competitive, they are likely to fail. Two specific deviations from perfect competition are considered here:

1. The problems of **monopoly**.
2. The immobility of factors of production (**immobile resources**).

The problems of monopoly

In a free market, there are two major reasons why monopolies might be expected to develop:

- **Economies of scale.** In many industries there are significant economies of scale available. This implies the need for firms to become large if they are to succeed in minimising their costs (a requirement of productive efficiency). The problem with this is that the market may not be able to sustain more than a few such large firms. In extreme cases, the market may only have room for one such large firm. This is the case of the **'natural monopoly'**.
- The **profit motive.** The key driving force behind the behaviour of producers in free markets is assumed to be the desire to achieve profits. The problem with this is that one of the most effective ways of making profit is to destroy competition. This allows firms to set their own prices and earn large profits that cannot be competed away by rivals.

It matters if there is a tendency towards monopolies in free markets because monopolies can be seen as leading to economic inefficiency and market failure. There is both allocative and productive inefficiency. This can be seen with reference to Figure 11, the standard monopoly diagram. The revenue schedules are downward-sloping as the firm has the power to set its own prices (unlike in perfect competition). The firm chooses to produce at the point where marginal cost is equal to marginal revenue as this is the level of production and sales that will secure maximum profit. This level of output Q_1 can be sold at a price of P_1, as suggested by the average revenue (or demand schedule). This implies that there is a supernormal profit equivalent to the shaded area. This level of profit will not be competed away in the long run as barriers to entry into the industry will prevent the entry of new firms.

- Allocative inefficiency. There is clearly allocative inefficiency in Figure 11 as at output Q_1 the selling price is greater than marginal cost. This implies that there is an under-production of the good or service: too few scarce resources are devoted to its production.
- Productive inefficiency. It can be seen from Figure 11 that there is technical inefficiency. The firm is not producing at the lowest point on its average cost curve. However, it cannot be seen whether the firm is producing on the lowest possible cost curve.

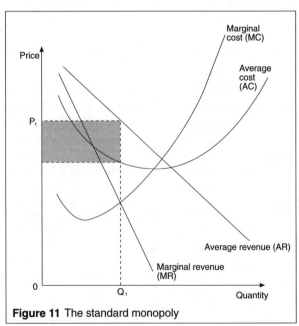

Figure 11 The standard monopoly

Byers orders competition reforms over milk prices

DAVID BROWN

Ministers ordered a big shake-up of the dairy industry after a Competition Commission report yesterday said consumers pay too much for milk. The commission found that Milk Marque, the co-operative owned by farmers which is Britain's largest milk supplier, had exploited its monopoly powers to raise the price of raw milk.

In a statement sending shock waves through the dairy farming industry Stephen Byers, Trade and Industry Secretary, demanded changes to Milk Marque's conditions of sale. He announced that Milk Marque will need the permission of the Director General of Fair Trading before any expansion to processing facilities to make cheese, yoghurts and other dairy products.

The commission, which investigated Milk Marque under its previous title, the Monopolies and Mergers Commission, concluded that any increase in processing by the co-operative 'may be expected to operate against the public interest by enhancing its ability to exploit its monopoly power'. Mr Byers rejected a recommendation to force the break-up of Milk Marque.

Milk Marque had a 49.6 per cent share of milk supplies after it replaced the defunct Milk Marketing Board for England and Wales in 1994. It now has 39 per cent. Under British rules, a business with more than 25 per cent of a market can be considered an unwelcome monopoly, but in Europe the cut-off point is 40 per cent.

The Daily Telegraph, 7 July 1999

The assumption is that monopolies will tend not to produce on their lowest possible cost curve due to the likelihood of 'x'-inefficiency. This is said to arise due to the lack of pressure on monopolists to control their costs and their ability to 'have an easy life'. Lack of competition means that a whole range of costs may be allowed to be higher than they have to be with monopolies because such behaviour is possible in a way that would lead to disaster in a competitive industry.

The article about the milk industry above points to the sort of economic problems created by monopolies. The suggestion made is that Milk Marque is charging 'too high' a price to consumers. It is able to do so because of its market power. Price is certainly judged to be above marginal cost and there is the likelihood that production costs are higher than they should be.

45

Immobile resources

One assumption of the perfectly competitive model is that all factors of production are perfectly mobile: they can be quickly and easily moved from one type of production to another. Often, this is seen not to be the case. Specifically with regard to labour, there may be both occupational and geographical immobility:

- **Occupational immobility.** Labour is said to be occupationally immobile if workers cannot easily move from one form of employment to another perhaps because they have the wrong skills. This creates a problem because the process by which the 'invisible hand' was seen to work in chapter 3 to accommodate changes in consumer preferences can no longer be seen to work in the way described. As consumers have shifted in their demand from food and non-alcoholic drinks to leisure services, workers should have swapped jobs accordingly. However, this may not have been possible as workers may not have possessed the necessary skills to make the move and may not easily have been able to acquire them. The result of this could be **structural unemployment**: workers stuck without jobs due to possessing the wrong skills. This is a very clear case of economic inefficiency. Scarce resources are not just being used appropriately: they are not being used at all. The economy is functioning inside its production possibility frontier.
- **Geographical immobility.** Workers may not only be required to move occupations due to a change in consumer preferences. They may also have to move locations. This will not happen if workers prove to be geographically immobile due to a range of possible barriers to geographical mobility. Such barriers could include social ties and the significantly different cost of housing in different parts of a country. The result of this could be **regional unemployment**. Regions associated with certain declining industries are left with unemployed workers who do not move to other parts of the country where new jobs exist in growing industries. Such unemployment is again a very clear example of economic inefficiency.

Conclusion

The conclusion of this chapter is to contradict the conclusion of chapter 3. There is a range of reasons why free markets left to their own devices may fail to deliver economic efficiency. Scarce resources may not be allocated in the optimum manner when markets operate freely. These market failures thus imply that there could be a case for the government to intervene in the operation of the economy in order to move the economy closer to a position of economic efficiency.

BEDE COLLEGE
HALE ROAD
BILLINGHAM
TS23 3ER

KEY WORDS

Market failure
Externality
Third party
Negative externality
Social cost
Private cost
External cost
Over-production
Road traffic congestion
Positive externality
Social benefit
Private benefit
External benefits
Under-production
Public goods
Non-excludability
Non-rivalry
Private goods
Free ride
Quasi-public goods

Imperfect information
Merit goods
De-merit goods
Inappropriate trades
Insurance markets
Paternalism
Positive Economics
Value judgements
Adverse selection
Moral hazard
Monopoly
Immobile resources
Economies of scale
Natural monopoly
Profit motive
'X'-inefficiency
Occupational immobility
Structural unemployment
Geographical immobility
Regional unemployment

Further reading

Begg, D. *et al.*, Chapter 15 in *Economics*, McGraw Hill, 5th edn, 1997.

Grant, S., Chapters 19–22 in *Stanlake's Introductory Economics*, 5th edn, Longman, 2000.

Lipsey, R. and Chrystal, A., Chapter 18 in *Principles of Economics*, Oxford University Press, 9th edn, 1999.

Sloman, J., Chapter 11 in *Economics*, Prentice Hall, 4th edn, 2000.

Useful websites

Adam Smith Institute: www.adamsmith.org.uk/policy/
Office of Fair Trading: www.oft.gov.uk.

Essay topics

1. (a) Distinguish between private, public and merit goods.
   [10 marks]
   (b) In 1987, the UK government abandoned its policy of providing free eye examinations for all patients. Use economic theory to discuss the likely effects of this policy decision.   [15 marks]
   [OCR, November, 1997]

2. (a) Using examples to illustrate your answer, explain what economists mean by 'market failure'.   [12 marks]
   (b) It is often argued that in the absence of government intervention, market failure will result in insufficient investment in vocational training. Assess the case for and against the government spending substantial sums of money to provide and encourage vocational training.   [13 marks]

Data response question

This task is based on a question set by the OCR exam board in 1997. Study the passage and table below, and then answer the questions that follow.

Cavalier Pet Products

Cavalier Pet Products is a large privately-owned manufacturer of canned pet foods based in Bolton, Lancashire. The company, which employs 300 people, is long-established and has been on its present site since it was founded by its owners, the Fazackerley family, in 1906. It is a market leader, producing own-branded products which are widely advertised and well known.

Through the nature of its manufacturing processes, the company is a polluter of the local environment. The nauseating smells from the factory, particularly in hot weather, are the main source of complaint; the firm also creates noise disturbance and quite recently was successfully prosecuted for discharging effluent into a local stream running alongside the factory. There is increasing local pressure from residents for something to be done about the whole question of the firm and its operations.

The obvious answer is for the firm to move to another location. The Managing Director of Cavalier Pet Foods, Basil Fazackerley, favours such a move but is quite adamant that 'we shall not pay the full cost. If the local council want us to move, then they will have to help us to do so.'

The decision to relocate the factory has long-term implications both for its owners and for the community. In particular, new jobs will be created as the firm increases output and the local environment within the vicinity of the present site will experience environmental gain.

The local authority have agreed to contribute to the relocation, as they can see a benefit to the community. Cavalier Pet Products remain concerned that they should pay a realistic contribution to the cost of relocation.

In order to sort out these difficulties, a local university was asked to carry out a 'cost-benefit' analysis of the proposed relocation. A summary of their findings is given in Table A below.

Table A Estimated discounted[1] costs and benefits of the relocation of Cavalier Pet Products (£000)

Costs		Benefits	
Private costs of the relocation	1,300	Private benefits	1,500
Contribution from local authority	300	External benefits	1,200
External costs	400		
Total costs	**2,000**	**Total benefits**	**2,700**

[1] Discounting is a procedure whereby a present value is given to costs and benefits that will occur some time in the future.

1. (a) Briefly state what is meant by a 'negative externality' and give *two* examples of negative externalities arising from the firm's operations at its *present* site. [6 marks]
   (b) Examine the consequences of these negative externalities for
   – the firm
   – the consumers of the firm's products
   – local residents. [9 marks]
2. Excluding relocation, explain what other methods might be proposed by economists in order to deal with the problems arising from the firm's operations. [10 marks]
3. (a) Use the information provided to demonstrate how cost-benefit analysis is taking a long view and a wide view of this project. [2 marks]
   (b) With reference to the proposed relocation, give an example of
   – a private benefit
   – an external benefit
   arising from the proposed relocation. Justify your choice.
   [6 marks]

4. Use Table A to state what conclusions you could draw from the cost-benefit analysis. [5 marks]

5. You are asked to plan an investigation to estimate the external costs and benefits of the relocation shown in Table A. Explain how you might do this and comment upon some of the problems you might foresee. [10 marks]

Chapter Five

Equity and efficiency

'*You cannot evaluate what's happening in an economy or a society without looking at people who are on the downside and not just those who are doing well and prospering.*'
Amartya Sen

'*The inherent vice of capitalism is the unequal sharing of blessings; the inherent virtue of socialism is the equal sharing of miseries.*'
Winston Churchill

Markets and inequality

A further concern arises about markets from the observation that they can lead to considerable **inequality**. Allowing markets to function in an entirely free fashion can lead to very unequal distributions of both **income** and **wealth** in a society.

- Income is defined as a flow of earnings over a specified period of time (often a year). It is the value of what a person earns.
- Wealth is defined as stock. It is the monetary value of everything possessed by a person at a given point in time. It is the value of what a person owns.

Clearly there is a relationship between wealth and income as income leads to the purchase of possessions that then contribute to wealth. However, there is an important difference insofar as wealth can be directly inherited whereas income cannot. Inequalities in wealth might thus give cause for a greater concern than inequalities in income.

The degree of inequality in incomes that can be generated by markets both between individuals in a society and between different societies is shown by the article below from *The Economist* regarding the high level of earnings of some of the top paid people in the United States.

Market economies also tend to generate considerable inequalities in wealth, a factor clearly resulting from inequalities in income according to a recent report from the Institute for Fiscal Studies about the United Kingdom reported in *The Independent* newspaper (see article on page 53). This is significant as the report considers a period of 20 years in the UK during which time there was a consistent

Who wants to be a billionaire?

Stock options have made many American bosses rich – but not necessarily any better at their jobs. No matter how good a chief executive may be, can he possibly be worth $200m? That is what Mel Karmazin, boss of CBS, a network company, in effect received last year – though only $9.8m of that took the form of salary and bonuses; all the rest came in stock options. Even his lucre was modest compared with the reward of Michael Eisner, head of Walt Disney: $576m, or roughly the GDP of the Seychelles, much of it acquired by realising vast option gains.

There has never been a better time to be the head of an American corporation. As a recent study of billionaires points out, America today has more of them relative to the size of the workforce than it had even in the early years of the century, when fortunes were made from railways and oil. Many of these billionaires are e-founders, the astonishingly youthful creators of Silicon Valley's successes. But the hired hands who run traditional big American business have also been accumulating wealth at an unprecedented pace. 'There's never been anything like the massive creation of fortunes that's happening now,' says Austan Goolsbee of the University of Chicago Business School.

The Economist, 8 May 1999

government economic policy to move more of the operation of the economy over to free market forces through such policies as **privatisation**.

Why the market leads to inequalities

The figures for the 1990s clearly suggest how unequal the **distribution** of wealth and income can become in market economies. The question is why this might happen. Economists can offer two reasons:

1. The forces of supply and demand.
2. Market imperfections.

Supply and demand

Income, or wages, can be seen as the price of labour. As such, income is determined, as with all prices, by the forces of supply of demand. A combination of high demand and low supply leads to high income; a combination of low demand and high supply will lead to low income. This is illustrated in Figure 12 on page 54.

The high level of demand of D_3 in Figure 12 when combined with the low level of supply of S_1 yields the high wage of W_1. The low

Average wealth climbs in Britain but distribution has grown more unequal

DIANE COYLE

Average wealth has climbed during the 1980s, but its distribution has grown more unequal, and the number of people with no **savings** at all has climbed.

Nearly 30 per cent of all Britons have no savings or investment outside their home and pension, and around 10 per cent have no savings at all, according to a new report from the Institute for Fiscal Studies. Most of this 10th consists of single parents and out-of-work couples.

Half the population has less than £750 in liquid savings – up from a figure of £455 in 1991/2. Most people still keep most of their money in a simple bank or building society account.

However, an average wealth of £7,136 compares with this median of £750, indicating that the distribution is very uneven. The Institute for Fiscal Studies reports that for the wealthiest 10th of the population, the average level of investments amounts to £50,000, and only the wealthiest quarter achieve an average level of more than £5,000.

The proportion of the population holding shares has increased significantly, up from less than one in 10 households at the beginning of the 1980s to more than one in five by the end of the decade.

The biggest increases in share ownership coincided with the privatisation of BT and British Gas.

The Independent, 22 October 1999

level of demand of D_1 combined with the high level of supply of S_3 gives the low wage of W_2. An understanding of why supply and demand may be high or low helps to understand why people's wages differ.

The wages of a highly paid football player may be understood in such a fashion:

- Demand is high because many people will pay a high price to see the final product produced by the footballer.
- The **productivity** of the top footballer could be judged to be high if he contributes significantly to the success of the football club.
- The supply of top footballers is very limited. Only a very few possess the **skills** sought after by top football clubs.

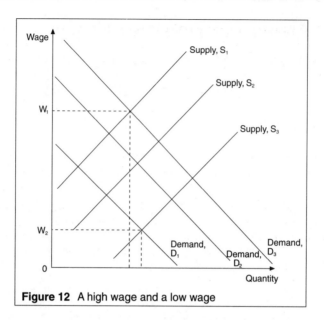

Figure 12 A high wage and a low wage

Market imperfections

The forces of supply and demand alone do not explain all income differentials. There are imperfections in the market that can also be seen as contributing towards inequality in incomes:

- **Barriers to entry.** There are barriers that prevent people entering certain occupations. These barriers help to restrict the supply of actual and potential workers and thus create a high wage. Barriers to entry could include any of the following: age, gender, race, social class and educational qualifications.
- **Bargaining power.** As markets become imperfect, then so the relative bargaining strength of employers and employees in different markets may explain why some wages are high and others are low. **Trade unions** could play a role in this. Some economists go further still and suggest that the whole power system in market economies is the key to understanding income differentials. **Karl Marx** suggested that everything really comes down to who owns the factor of production of capital and who does not. Those who did would earn large incomes as they were able to control the market system. Those who did not would never earn large incomes as they were at the mercy of the **capitalists** running the whole production system.

Does inequality in free markets matter?

Given that free markets appear to create significant inequalities, the question must be asked as to whether this matters. In general, inequality is seen to matter when it is associated with inequity or 'unfairness'. A **value judgement** is often made that it is not right and fair that there should be large variations in wealth and income especially in the same society. This is especially true when it is felt that one person's income is seen to be generated at the expense of others as in the case of the report from *The Daily Mirror*. The sense of 'unfairness' or inequity is made strongly in the article.

The point about the inequity of unequal distributions of income and wealth can also be made by recalling the argument that market economies are the equivalent of political democracies. The problem with this suggestion is that the voting system is not the same. In a political democracy, everyone has the same number of votes. This is not true in the so-called 'economic democracy'. Here the number of votes varies greatly between individuals depending upon the incomes

Oliver Twist 2000

Scrooge bosses are paying their staff Dickensian wages in the run-up to Christmas, it was claimed last night.

Wages watchdogs are investigating claims that the rate at an electronics factory is as little as £1.65 an hour.

More than 150 **home workers** rely on the Ebbw Vale based E-cam Technology for pin money in one of Wales' biggest unemployment blackspots. The workers take electronic components home to assemble and are paid by the bag load. They can earn £16.50, £15.60 or £12.00, depending on the size of the bag.

The company asks them to sign an agreement to say the work takes them four hours. On that basis the home workers would be paid above the legal £3.60 an hour minimum wage set last April.

But some workers claim they can spend as much as 10 hours finishing the largest bag of components, pushing their earnings down to pitiful levels.

Last night Labour AM [Member of the Welsh Assembly] Andrew Davies, who is campaigning to name and shame Scrooge employers, called the pay-outs disgusting. But he admitted that his hands were tied because of an official loop-hole.

Andrew Davies blasted the low-wage bosses. He said: 'Charles Dickens first talked about Scrooge employers 100 years ago. Here we are on the cusp of a new millennium and they are still here. The minimum wage law was brought in to help people on lower incomes.'

Last night DTI boss Alan Johnson said: 'The Government has always identified home workers as being particularly vulnerable to exploitation.'

The Daily Mirror, 23 December 1999

commanded by different people. Equality is the hallmark of political democracies but inequality is the hallmark of economic democracies.

Value judgements

Economists find themselves in a difficult area with such discussions because we are very clearly in the territory of significant value judgements. Who is to say what is 'fair' or 'unfair'? What is equitable and what is inequitable? These are significant and important issues but ones that many economists feel uncomfortable in tackling. In theory, **positive economics** avoids value judgements. These tend to be left to philosophers, politicians and the man or woman in the street.

Certainly the notion of equality lies outside the definitions of economic efficiency considered in chapter 2:

- Allocative efficiency takes the distribution of income as given without making any judgements about it. A change in the starting distribution of income would lead to a different allocation of resources (as different individuals have different preferences) and this could also be judged to be allocatively efficient.
- Pareto efficiency similarly simply accepts the starting income distribution and proceeds from there. It makes no comment or judgement upon that initial distribution.

The role of the economist in this is traditionally seen as identifying and clarifying income and wealth differentials for interested parties (such as politicians) and identifying the effects of any government policies upon these differentials. No judgements are made upon the desirability of the different possible distributions.

Social effects

A further concern about significant inequality in wealth and income may arise from the possible undesirable social effects of the perceived inequity. Very unequal societies are unlikely to be socially harmonious ones. At the most extreme level, they may be ones in danger of rebellion and uprising if the 'have-nots' feel that the inequity is too great to accept. This is the sort of concern sometimes expressed about the state of some Eastern European societies after the fall of **communism**. The ensuing free market system is seen as generating such an unacceptable situation that many people now hanker after earlier communist days.

Are equity and efficiency incompatible?

An important final point in this consideration of **equity** and the free market system is whether significant inequality in income (and thus probably wealth) are a necessary (if perhaps unfortunate) requirement for the successful operation of such a system.

The key to the success of free markets is often seen to be the **incentives** that they create. This was seen to be the case in chapter 3 where the profit motive was seen as leading firms to produce the right products in the right way so that economic efficiency resulted:

- The desire for profit-led producers to produce exactly those products most wanted by consumers. This produced allocative efficiency.
- The motive of profit was the driving force in ensuring that firms minimised their costs. This gave productive efficiency.

Thus, the possibility of earning significant profits must be there if resources are to be used well. Similarly, individual workers need the incentive, so it is argued, to work hard and develop their skills. This will help to ensure that the maximum production is forthcoming from the factor of production of labour. It implies the need for unequal incomes so that workers can work towards earning higher incomes.

A further need for inequality in incomes comes from the working of the 'invisible hand'. Chapter 3 described how workers would ideally move from one occupation to another in response to changes in consumer preferences and technology. To do this, they need the appropriate **signals**. These signals are provided by rising and falling wages. Workers will then leave industries with falling wages and join industries with rising wages.

Market economies must, then, be characterised by some inequality in income (and hence probably wealth) if they are to function effectively and lead to economic efficiency. The question, however, must be how much inequality is needed or is optimal. This is not an easy question to answer. There are reasons for suggesting, however, that the **optimum level of inequality** may well be less than the level that could be generated by entirely free markets:

- The existence of supernormal profit suggests that producers sometimes receive greater income than is needed to induce them to undertake their current operations. The lack of competition enables them to receive high profits that are not economically justified. Income is more unequal than it needs to be. Similarly, there are people receiving high wages for their current employment (possibly such as the top football player mentioned earlier) when they would be prepared to continue in the same line of employment for a lower income. Again, income is more unequal than it needs to be.

- If the resource of labour is to be effectively used, it needs to be in good health and as productive as possible. This suggests the desirability of education and health care up to a certain level for all regardless of income levels. This can be understood in the context of education and health care being products that have positive externalities. They will be under-produced in the free market and unavailable to those on very low incomes.

Conclusion

The suggestion that is often made about market economies is that they do not provide equity. There are forces at work in markets that can lead to very unequal distributions of both wealth and income. This is therefore often seen as another reason why governments need to intervene in the running of the economy. The problem is that there is never likely to be clear agreement on what is the ideal level of inequality in society. Economists have the role of suggesting the possible impact upon distribution of different economic policies. Politicians and voters then decide what policy to adopt.

KEY WORDS

Inequality	Karl Marx
Income	Capitalists
Wealth	Value judgements
Stock (share) options	Home workers
Privatisation	Positive economics
Distribution	Communism
Savings	Equity
Productivity	Incentives
Skills	(Market) signals
Barriers to entry	Optimum level of inequality
Bargaining power	Market reforms
Trade unions	

Further reading

Grant, S and Vidler, C., Advanced Section 2 Unit 5 in *Economics in Context*, Heinemann, 2000.

Griffiths, A. and Wall, S., Chapter 14 in *Applied Economics*, Pearson, 8th edn, 1999.

Simpson, L. and Paterson, I., Chapter 4 in *The UK Labour Market*, Heinemann, 1995.

Sloman, J., Chapter 10 in *Economics*, Prentice Hall, 4th edn, 2000.

Essay topics
1. Traditionally, university education in the UK has been subsidised, with tuition fees paid by the state.
(a) Explain why university education in the UK is regarded as a merit good. [10 marks]
(b) Discuss the likely economic effects on the market for university education of requiring students to pay £1000 per year towards tuition fees. [15 marks]
[OCR, March 1999]
2. (a) Explain why inequalities in income are a necessary requirement for the successful operation of a market system.
[12 marks]
(b) Discuss the extent to which such inequalities in income are a necessary requirement for the successful operation of a market system. [13 marks]

Useful websites
Income Data Services: www.incomedata.co.uk
Low Pay Unit: www.lowpay.gov.uk/
Office for National Statistics (ONS): www.ons.gov.uk/

Data response question
This task is based on a question set by the OCR exam board for its Market System and Market Failure paper for March 2000. Study the passage, figure and extract below and then answer the questions that follow.

Labour market failure in London

The labour market is a good example of a market where the forces of supply and demand do not operate as expected by economic theory. A particular illustration of this market failure is in London where there are thousands of unfilled vacancies in hotels, restaurants and catering outlets (see Extract A). These activities invariably pay low wages, often to students and casual workers, and are typical of the employers being targeted by the government's announcement of a national minimum wage of £3.60 per hour from April 1999. Workers under 21 years old and receiving some form of training can be paid a lower rate.

Economists have analysed the effects of introducing such a minimum wage. Figure A below, which assumes a perfectly competitive labour market, shows the effects of introducing a national minimum wage on low-pay occupations such as in hotels, restaurants and catering. The demand curve (D) represents the number of hours of labour that firms will wish to buy at various wage rates; the supply curve (S) shows the number of hours that workers will be willing to work at various wage rates.

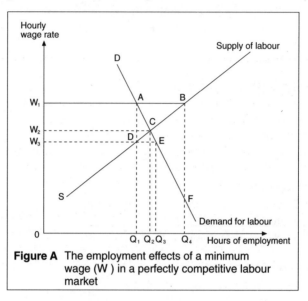

Figure A The employment effects of a minimum wage (W) in a perfectly competitive labour market

Extract A
Joining the Foreign Service

London now has more restaurants per head than any other city and the hospitality industry (as hotels, restaurants and catering outlets are now called) is the second largest employer in Britain. Many are small businesses, although, increasingly, large national and international operators account for the £2 billion spent by London's 27m tourists on food and drink.

There is a serious shortage of 'waiting staff' in London. So much so, in fact, that more and more such staff are foreign and young, despite information on vacancies not being easily accessible to prospective workers. Many employers are more than happy to employ foreign staff, not least because Britons do not like serving each other. One section of British society still willing to wait at tables though are ex-public school pupils and other students from middle class backgrounds. They seem more prepared to work, at least temporarily, for low wages and usually have more initiative in seeking appropriate opportunities in comparison with other types of casual labour.

One restaurateur, Laurence Isaacson of Chez Gerard, thinks that it will be difficult to find the 2000 staff needed to cater for those who want to eat and drink in the Millennium Dome.

Source: adapted from *The Daily Telegraph*, 18 August 1998

1. (a) State *four* characteristics of a 'perfectly competitive market'.
    [4 marks]
    (b) Use the material in Extract A to analyse the extent to which the market for 'waiting staff' in London is a perfectly competitive *labour market*. [4 marks]
2. With reference to Figure A:
    (a) At which point is the labour market in equilibrium? Explain what this means. [2 marks]
    (b) Describe the slope of the supply curve for labour and explain its significance for restaurant owners. [2 marks]
    (c) *Excluding hourly wage rates*, stage and explain *two* other factors which might determine the supply of 'waiting staff' to London's restaurants. [4 marks]
3. 'There is a serious shortage of waiting staff in London (Extract A, Line 7). Explain how this is represented in Figure A.
    [4 marks]
4. With the aid of a diagram, explain how the wage rates of 'waiting staff' in London might be affected by the opening of the Millennium Dome. [4 marks]
5. The average wage rate for 'waiting staff' in London in 1998 was £3 per hour.
    (a) Use Figure A to explain how the introduction of a national minimum wage of £3.60 per hour might affect the employment of 'waiting staff'. [4 marks]
    (b) State and explain *two* possible reasons why some workers under 21 years old have been excluded from the minimum wage legislation. [4 marks]
6. You are required to plan an investigation into the likely effects of the introduction of a minimum wage on the demand for and supply of 'waiting staff' in London. What information would you need to collect and how might you obtain it? [8 marks]
7. Comment upon the likely short and long term effects on the restaurant industry in London of introducing the national minimum wage legislation. [10 marks]

Chapter Six

Government intervention

'It is not my intention to do away with government. It is rather to
make it work . . . work with us, not over us; stand by our side, not
ride on our back. Government can and must provide opportunity,
not smother it; foster productivity, not stifle it.'
Ronald Reagan (1981)

'Government's view of the economy could be summed up in a few
short phrases: If it moves, tax it. If it keeps moving, regulate it. And
if it stops moving, subsidise it.'
Ronald Reagan (1986)

If markets are seen to fail, the question then arises as to what should
be done. Is it possible to move the economy closer to economic efficiency than could be the case if everything is left to the market? The
answer is that the government can try to intervene in order to improve
the level of economic efficiency.

Purpose of intervention
The purpose of **government intervention** *is to overcome market failures.* The economic justification for government policies is that
market failures are present and thus resources are not being used in
the ideal or optimum fashion. Governments can then try to introduce
policies that will overcome the inefficiencies present in the market
and lead to a better use of scarce resources. This chapter looks at
some of the policies available to governments and considers how they
can be used in an effort to overcome the market failures outlined in
chapter 4 as well as the concerns about the distribution of wealth
and income considered in chapter 5.

Taxes and subsidies
The government can use both **taxes** and **subsidies** to affect the level
of production and consumption of a product and thus move production and consumption closer to the optimal level.
  *The purpose of a tax is to discourage production of a product that
is over-produced by the market.*
  *The purpose of a subsidy is to encourage production of a product
that is under-produced by the market.*

Taxation

The type of tax used in this way will be an **indirect tax**. A tax is imposed on the producer of the product and that producer may, to some extent, be able to pass on that tax burden to the final consumer.

An obvious use of taxation would be on goods and services that are seen to produce negative externalities. The aim of the government is to set a tax upon the producer equal to the value of the negative externality associated with producing the product. This forces the producer to pay the full social costs of production and thus moves the market towards the optimal level of production. This is illustrated in Figure 13 where the free market equilibrium is shown by quantity Q_1 and price P_1. This is the point where marginal private cost is equal to marginal social benefit (or average revenue or demand). The problem with this, as seen in chapter 4, is that it represents an overproduction because social costs are greater than private costs. The government can thus attempt to impose a tax equal to the value of the negative externality and thus shift the private cost schedule so that it becomes equal to the social cost schedule. In this way **the externality is said to be 'internalised'**. The producer is forced to pay it. This amount is illustrated by the vertical distance 't' in Figure 13. If a tax of 't' is imposed on each unit of production, then the marginal private cost schedule is shifted to the level of the marginal social cost

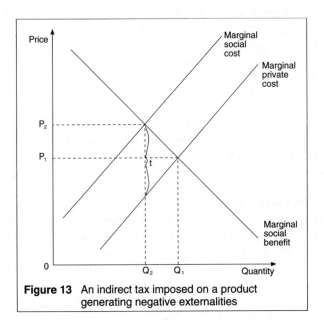

Figure 13 An indirect tax imposed on a product
generating negative externalities

schedule and thus there is a new equilibrium level of production and consumption of Q_2 with a new price of P_2. This has moved the market to the optimal production point and stopped the over-production.

There are many possible examples of such taxes (sometimes referred to as 'sin taxes') being used by a government. Until leaded petrol was finally banned in the UK from the beginning of 2000, it was taxed at a higher rate than unleaded petrol in recognition of the negative externality of the greater **environmental damage** created by leaded petrol compared to unleaded petrol.

Schemes for **road charges** can be seen as the same type of policy. The negative externality of road congestion was seen as leading to an over-use of road transport in chapter 4. The remedy here would be to charge road users an amount equal to the external cost that they were creating by using the road. This raises the issue of measuring the right amount to charge. With traffic congestion, this would certainly mean varying charges during the day as traffic congestion varies during the day. The article about the scheme to introduce road charges in Leicester in the UK below indicates both how such schemes might be introduced and how the issue of charging the appropriate amount is an important one. The suggestion is that once a certain charge is reached there will be a significant impact upon road use; before that point, there will be little impact. Two other important points can be noted from the article:

- The intention is to reduce the use of cars not to eliminate it. This fits in with the relevant economic theory that suggests that there is over-production rather than that *all* production is undesirable.
- There is a further charge planned when car use is clearly contributing to pollution. This is the same principle of attempting to introduce a charge to match the negative externality produced.

Taxation of this sort could also be considered to be an appropriate policy to deal with de-merit goods. Again, the problem is seen to be one of over-production and thus a tax of the appropriate level could deter consumption and production so that it is reduced to a more appropriate level. This might justify the large tax imposed by governments, such as in the UK, on cigarettes. Such taxes may reduce the amount of smoking to a level closer to the level if consumers had full information about the impact of its consumption. The case with cigarettes is complicated as the tax can also be justified in terms of the negative externalities that smokers could be deemed to impose in the form of secondary smoking and costs to the health service of smoking related diseases.

Road tolls 'must be set at £6 a day to deter drivers'

PAUL MARSTON

Road tolls will need to be set at about £6 a day if they are to deter commuters from travelling to work by car, according to results from a Government-sponsored trial.

Preliminary findings from Britain's first 'pay-as-you-drive' experiment also indicate that ministers risk generating widespread unpopularity if they press ahead with tolls when the transport White Paper is published next spring. John Prescott, Deputy Prime Minister, has made clear that he views road tolling as potentially one of the most powerful weapons for reducing the use of cars and encouraging demand for public transport.

The pilot scheme has taken place in Leicester since September, with a representative sample of regular drivers being charged a notional £3 a day to take their cars into the city centre between 7 am and 10 am. As they enter the pricing area, an overhead beacon electronically registers the toll on a pre-paid smartcard unit fixed to the windscreen behind the rear view mirror. The driver hears a bleep as the money is deducted.

However, if the participants choose to leave their car at a park-and-ride area on the edge of the city centre and proceed by bus, they are charged only £1.30.

While the daily charge was left at £3, it was found that 80 per cent of the 110 participants remained in their cars, with 15 per cent using the park-and-ride and five per cent arranging lifts or walking.

But the effect of raising the toll in mid-November to £6 has been dramatic. The proportion sticking with the car has dropped to less than 50 per cent, with park-and-ride users estimated to have risen to more than a third.

Jonathan Smith, of the Transport Research Laboratory, stressed that the aim of the trial was not to pitch tolls so high that cars disappeared from the road, as that was 'not practical' as a policy measure. He said: 'We would like to shift about 30 per cent of drivers. That would make a big difference to traffic and the environment.'

A lower toll of £4 is to be tried from 5 January between 7.30 and 9.30 in the morning, with those travelling within 90 minutes of the peak band facing a £2 charge. This is to attempt to assess price-sensitivity more precisely, and to see how many drivers will change their normal working time to pay a lesser charge.

A further refinement is planned for days of poor air quality, when the normal toll will be doubled to reduce the impact of pollution in the centre of Leicester.

The Daily Telegraph, 26 December 1997

Subsidies

Subsidies work in the opposite way to indirect taxes. The government gives producers money in order to encourage the production of a product. This would thus be seen as a relevant policy in the case both of products with positive externalities and with merit goods. Both of these categories of goods and services are under-produced by the free market and thus there is a case for encouraging their production to a point closer to the optimal production level.

The impact of a subsidy on a free market for a product with positive externalities can be seen in Figure 14. The market equilibrium is where the marginal cost schedule cuts the average private benefit schedule. This gives a consumption and production level of Q_1 with a price of P_1. The impact of the government subsidy is to reduce the costs of production and thus lower the marginal cost schedule. This causes the level of production to rise, in the case of Figure 14 to quantity Q_2. This has increased the level of production to the optimal level where the average social benefit is equal to the original marginal cost schedule.

Subsidies might be justified for any products that are seen to have positive externalities or are deemed to be merit goods. Education would thus seem to be a clear candidate for government subsidies under both categories. It is interesting to note, however, that **free provision** is not obviously advocated. This is because there is some private benefit from the product for which consumers might be expected to pay. Unlike a public good, a merit good *will* be provided

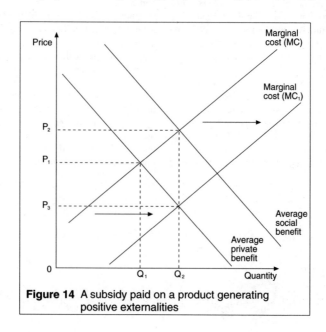

Figure 14 A subsidy paid on a product generating positive externalities

by the free market: it will simply be under-provided. However, most developed countries do provide education to most children free of charge to the user.

Subsidies might also be paid to consumers as well as producers. An example of this is the payment available to households for insulating their homes so that energy is more efficiently used. The reason for doing this is the same as subsidising the producer and is intended to have the same results.

Any product that is thought to have significant benefits to society is seen as a potential contender for a government subsidy. This is the case with solar power in the article by Polly Toynbee below. The criteria as to whether a subsidy can be justified should be whether such a product has positive externalities associated with it and/or can be seen as a merit good. A further argument here appears to be that initial production must be subsidised so that **economies of scale** can reduce the costs of all subsequent production.

The use of subsidies could also be justified in further ways:

- Some of the problems of the geographical immobility of labour might be overcome by offering subsidies to firms to set up production in areas of high unemployment, thus helping to overcome the inefficiency of unemployed scarce resources. This is the basis of most governments' **regional policies**.
- The **training and re-training of labour**. This could help to overcome the problems created by occupational immobility. Subsidising training could also be justified insofar as it generates positive externalities. Other firms may well benefit from the training if an employee moves to another firm.
- The **redistribution of income**. Subsidies might be seen as increasing the incomes of those on low incomes. This is seen as part of the justification for the subsidisation of agriculture in the European Union.

Government provision and cost-benefit analysis

The government might go beyond subsidising the production of a good or service and decide to produce it itself. Common examples of such **government provision** in developed economies might be:

- education
- health care
- defence
- emergency services
- infrastructure (roads, street lighting, sewerage systems, etc.).

Solar power is clean, cheap and catching fire abroad

Polly Toynbee

Among the multitudinous predictions about the next century, this one is a near certainty: unless the government acts at once Britain will miss out on the next great industrial revolution. Solar energy is destined to power the next century but Britain will not cash in on the vast new industry manufacturing it. Clean, inexhaustible, universally available, this technology is the next century's equivalent of the microchip. But as solar energy bursts upon the world, yet again Britain will be left behind.

In a decade or two under any palm tree, beside any fjord, on any steppe or savannah thousands of miles from a power line, people will sit down with a few panels and access the world on a computer, power any machine or well, heat or cool themselves with no more than the light of the sun. Clean, renewable energy for industry will be there for the taking – but not from panels made in Britain.

America, Japan and Germany are already constructing huge production plants for manufacturing solar panels. They will soon achieve economies of scale that will bring the price of solar energy tumbling down. It requires strong government investment in these early uneconomic stages, support given liberally by foreign governments in direct subsidy and **tax incentives** to early purchasers – but not by the Department of Trade and Industry. As a result BP and Shell have moved their solar energy industries out of Britain to the US and Holland.

So far in Britain without the subsidies, tax incentives and **interest free loans** offered abroad, the main economic use for solar energy is for powering rural bus shelters or farms far from electricity supplies. Typically a farmer quoted £35,000 to be connected to mains electricity two miles away finds solar panels cost only £28,000, with free energy thereafter.

The Kyoto **carbon reduction targets** are already too little too late and even they won't be met. With the rapid coal-driven industrialisation of China and India, the west's ability to offer those countries cheap solar technology instead could be the saving of the world. But the only way for the price to come down is by widespread development of it at home.

The Guardian, 29 December 1999

The system used by governments in the above examples is to finance the production through the tax system and then to provide the goods or services free (or nearly free) of charge to consumers.

The failure of the market to guarantee the production of public goods is a possible justification for government provision. Chapter 4 explained how public goods might not be produced by the free market due to the problem of 'free riding'. The solution then could be for the government to provide the product that the market cannot and to raise the necessary finance through the taxation system. This leads to desirable production taking place. It can explain the government provision of such items as a national defence system, street lighting and sewerage systems. They could all be deemed to be examples of public goods.

It is important to note that not all of the products provided by the government are examples of public goods. The most notable two are health care and education. These services do not meet the two necessary criteria of non-excludability and non-rivalry. They would be provided (if in insufficient quantity) by the market. As merit goods, they would be under-provided, but they would still be provided in a free market. The justification for government (nearly) free provision funded through the tax system must therefore lie elsewhere. The only possible answer is that it links with the concerns expressed in chapter 5 over the distribution of income and wealth in a market economy. One means of reducing inequality is to provide certain **universally used services** free of charge to all. Higher income earners then pay for most of the provision as they are the highest tax-payers. A judgement has been made in most developed economies that every individual has a 'right' to education and health care and that the way to ensure this is to provide a certain level of service free to all citizens.

Once the government enters the area of providing goods and services complications arise. There are decisions to be made about:

- what to provide
- how much to provide.

The second issue is similar to the problems involved in setting an indirect tax at the right level to generate the 'correct' level of production. The first issue leads to difficult questions such as 'Should a new hospital or a new school be built in a town?' Which of three possible new roads should be built?' It is in order to tackle such problems that governments may resort to a technique called **'cost-benefit analysis'**. *Cost-benefit analysis is a means of comparing the social costs of a project with the social benefits in order to inform decision-making.*

If the government decides that it wishes to provide a public good or service, then it must have some means of judging between alternative possibilities. By using cost-benefit analysis, a government can compare the relative desirability of different means of spending taxpayers' money and make the decision that leads to the greatest net contribution to **economic welfare**. The way that this is judged is to opt for the alternative that yields the greatest surplus of social benefit over social cost.

The decision about building a new road would be a clear possibility for the use of cost-benefit analysis. The government may see the need for developing a new road in a particular part of the country. However, there are three alternative routes. How does it decide between them? The answer is to add up the monetary value of all the possible social costs and social benefits of the different projects. This must include both the private and external costs and benefits. This will allow a comparison of the overall **net social benefit** of the different routes.

Such a technique is not without difficulty. Most notably, it is very difficult to place a **monetary value** on some costs and benefits:

- This is particularly true with external costs and benefits. What is the precise value of the reduced pollution in one area compared to the increased noise and loss of scenery in another area?
- Even more controversially, how can the value of five less lives lost each year on one scheme compare with the loss of eight less lives each year on another scheme? The implication here is the need to place a monetary **value on a human life,** something that many people judge undesirable and impossible to do. There are various ways of attempting this, such as the **principle of 'willingness to pay'** that asks people how much they would be willing to pay to reduce the risk of death from one probability to another. This can generate a figure for the value of a fraction of a life which can then be converted into the value of a whole life.
- Valuing costs and benefits in the future presents a further problem. Should they have exactly the same value as current costs and benefits or should their value be viewed as less significant? If the latter is true, a **discounting technique** is needed so as to be able to compare costs and benefits in different time periods.

The article on page 72 about cost-benefit analyses of different road schemes in the UK shows both how they can be used and how they can be controversial. Once the market has been abandoned, there is no easy decision-making process.

Price controls

A government may decide that the market-determined price of a product is inappropriate and thus it will impose certain prices upon a market (**price controls**). It may impose either a **minimum price** or a **maximum price.**

A minimum price does not permit the market price to fall below a certain level. Its effect can be seen in Figure 15.

The market-determined price is given by P_1 where supply is equal to demand. However, the government decides that this is too low and thus it insists that price cannot be permitted to fall below P_{min}. At this price, producers supply a quantity of Q_3 but consumers demand only Q_2. Thus there is a **surplus** of Q_2Q_3.

There are two notable examples of minimum prices used by governments:

- The minimum price for agricultural produce in the European Union. This is imposed to protect the livelihoods of farmers both for reasons of income distribution and wider concerns about the desirability of maintaining an agricultural sector in EU countries. As suggested by Figure 15, it has led to large surpluses of certain products.
- The **minimum wage** in many developed countries. This has been introduced by governments for reasons of equity, as suggested in chapter 5. It is a means of ensuring that paid employment always generates a certain income level. Clearly, there are concerns that it could create a surplus of labour (or **unemployment**). However, this is dependent upon the labour market being highly competitive, as represented by a supply and demand diagram. In practice, many employers may be earning supernormal profits that can be re-distributed to workers without creating unemployment.

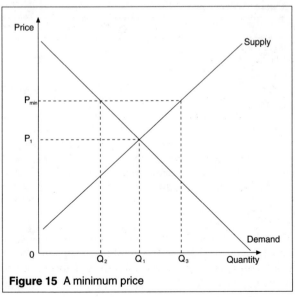

Figure 15 A minimum price

Ministers put brakes on best-value road schemes

PAUL MARSTON

Nearly a third of the road-building schemes approved by the Government will deliver smaller benefits in reduced congestion and safety than projects that were rejected, according to an analysis by civil servants.

Advice seen by ministers before the roads review was announced two months ago shows that 16 of the 37 improvements eventually given the go-ahead represented relatively poor value for money in terms of their likely transport advantages during the next 30 years.

The 16, costing £744 million, were all assessed as having 'benefit-cost ratios' of less than 3.0. Yet 13 others with higher ratings and a slightly lower price-tag were abandoned or deferred. The ratios were arrived at by estimating the value of the savings a scheme will achieve and dividing it by the cost of the building.

Roads: poor value decisions

Three improvements given the go-ahead

Scheme	Cost, £m	Benefit/cost ratio	Decision
A2/A282 Dartford, Kent	38	1.5	Approved
A500 Hough/Shavington bypass, Cheshire	28	1.7	Approved
A6 Clapham bypass, Beds.	31	1.95	Approved

Three that were turned down

Scheme	Cost, £m	Benefit/cost ratio	Decision
A4 Waggoners/Henlys Corner, nr. Heathrow	14	25.0	Dropped
M1 widening between J31–32, S. Yorks.	6	11.0	Shelved
A406/A1/A598 junction N. London	106	8.7	Shelved

Though the review as a whole provides scant evidence of political bias, two of the lowest-scoring approved schemes raised some eyebrows at Westminster. One was the A500 Hough/Shavington bypass in the constituency of Gwyneth Dunwoody, Chairman of the Transport Select Committee. The second was the Bingley relief road in Shipley, west Yorks, where Labour has one of its narrowest majorities.

Ministers say their decisions were based on environmental factors in addition to safety and economy, but some of the rejected schemes scored as well on these criteria as those that are proceeding.

The Daily Telegraph, 29 September 1998

A maximum price does not allow the market price to rise above a certain level. The government may make a decision that the market-determined price is too high and must be lowered. The obvious case for this is with monopolies where price could be set at a high level (above marginal cost and yielding significant supernormal profit) and thus the government insists that it is lower. This can be seen as achieving two desirable goals:

- Moving price closer to marginal cost.
- Redistributing some supernormal profit to consumers.

This is the policy employed by the UK government for regulating large **privatised monopolies** such as water, gas, electricity and telecommunications. The regulators order a certain price and these industries have to comply.

Legal controls

Another weapon open to the government in the face of market failure is to use the force of the law. Certain actions can be outlawed or forced in order to overcome possible undesirable market outcomes. There are many examples of governments doing this. The following represent just a few:

- All children have to attend school between certain ages in many countries. This stops under-consumption due to imperfect information about the benefits of education.
- Everyone travelling in a car in the UK must wear a seatbelt. This stops people not using seatbelts due to a lack of information about the benefits. It also reduces the health care costs associated with a failure to wear seatbelts.
- Traffic is now banned from some city centres. This reduces the negative externalities of pollution and accidents.
- Various **monopoly practices** are illegal. This might include such things as **price-fixing** and deliberate attempts to destroy competition, things that take the market further away from a position of economic efficiency. Companies with monopoly power may have rules imposed upon them that would not be there in a free market. This is the case with the example of the telecommunication regulator **OFTEL** insisting that BT allows other smaller companies access to its **infrastructure** (see newspaper article below).

Legal controls clearly represent a very strong intervention in the market. They can be seen as a different policy to taxes and subsidies that attempt to work with the market and move it to a different

Oftel plans to end BT's local call monopoly

Robert Uhlig

All phone calls could soon be charged at a flat monthly rate irrespective of destination, duration and frequency after Oftel said yesterday that it would end BT's monopoly of the local network.

Proposals by Oftel would allow BT's rivals access to its last stranglehold, the wires, called the local loop, that connect homes and businesses to local telephone exchanges. Experts believe that the proposals, which Oftel calls 'the most important decision in recent years', will lead to a revolution in telecommunications services.

They would allow companies such as Energis, Colt and MCI Worldcom access to the home without having to build their own infrastructure as cable television companies have done. BT still controls access to more than 80 per cent of homes. Several data services are promised, such as interactive television, films on demand and access to the Internet at vastly higher speeds than at present.

The proposals require BT to allow rivals access by July 2001. It can either invest significantly in its network and switches, and then lease the improved lines to its competitors, or it must allow them access to its local network so that they can upgrade it.

BT, which insiders said is furious at the proposals, stated that it favoured the first proposal. It has announced that it will invest £5 billion to transform ordinary telephone lines into high-speed digital channels to the Internet and other multi-media services.

The Daily Telegraph, 7 July 1999

position while still allowing producers and consumers to make choices within the market. Legal controls over-rule the free market outcome and disallow certain behaviours.

Information provision

In chapter 4, it was suggested that the free market sometimes failed due to imperfect information. Given this, there would seem to be a potential role for the government in the provision of information so that these failures are reduced. The sorts of possibilities are as follows:

- Forcing consumers in insurance markets to give proper information to insurers. In insurance markets, this is known as the principle of acting 'in **good faith**'. It is illegal for consumers not to declare all relevant information when attempting to become insured. This may help to overcome the problem of 'adverse selection'.

- Advertising standards. Advertisers have to be truthful in the claims made about their products. A failure to do so could result in prosecution. This should stop undesirable trades occurring due to consumers receiving inaccurate information about products through advertising.
- **Information provision** about merit and de-merit goods that indicate the true level of benefits of the product. This would include the health warnings that are given about cigarettes in all cigarette advertising. This is the sort of belief expressed in the article below about the costs of smoking, that if people truly understood the associated costs, then the level of smoking would decrease. However, it may also indicate the dangers of dictating what is 'good' for a person given the statement by the 'Right to smoke' organisation.

Smokers 'lose 11 minutes for each cigarette'

CHERRY NORTON

Every cigarette smoked cuts life expectancy by 11 minutes, bringing death six and a half years sooner for a regular smoker, says new research.

Researchers from the University of Bristol have found that if a man smokes an average 16 cigarettes a day from the age of 17 until his death at 71, he will have consumed 311,688 cigarettes by the time he dies. As the average life expectancy is six and a half years less than for a non-smoker, each cigarette costs him 11 minutes of his life.

Dr Mary Shaw, of the School of Geographical Sciences at the University of Bristol, who is author of the letter containing the research, published in the

British Medical Journal today, said that although the calculation was crude it 'shows the high cost of smoking in a way that everyone can understand'.

Government figures show that although 70 per cent of smokers say they want to give up, many struggle to do so. Smoking directly causes 46,000 cancer deaths each year and 40,000 from heart disease.

Martin Ball, spokesman of the Freedom Organisation for the Right to Enjoy Smoking Tobacco, said: 'What can you do with 11 minutes? Boil the kettle three times. Adults in a Western democracy have the right to make their own choice and smoke tobacco.'

The Independent, 31 December 1999

Progressive taxation and cash benefits

There are two further major ways in which the government can intervene in the running of the economy in order to reduce income inequalities if society judges the outcomes of the free market to be inequitable.

A **progressive tax** *is one that charges higher income earners a higher proportion of their incomes than lower income earners.* If such taxes are used, the net impact is that post-tax income is less unequal than pre-tax income. This can be easily illustrated by a **Lorenz curve**, as in Figure 16.

The Lorenz curve shows how the nation's income is distributed among the nation's population. A perfectly even distribution of income would lead to a straight 45-degree line in the manner indicated. The further the line deviates from this, the greater the level of income inequality in society. Figure 16 shows that a progressive tax system leads to a more equal income distribution.

The usual progressive tax that is used in developed economies is income tax. Usually, as in the UK, there is more than one rate of tax with the marginal rate of tax rising for higher income earners.

Cash benefits are another simple means of redistributing income in society. There are two types of benefits that are paid:

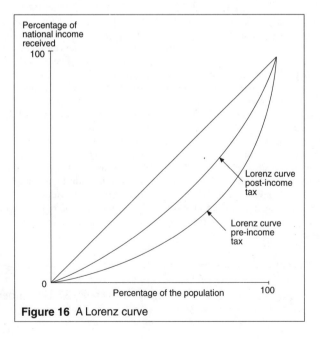

Figure 16 A Lorenz curve

- **Means-tested benefits.** These benefits are available only for people who qualify for them in terms of having low incomes. Benefits paid to those unemployed would be an obvious example. The advantage of these benefits are that they are clearly targeted at those who have low incomes. It is not 'wasted' on those who do not need it.
- **Universal benefits.** These benefits are paid to everyone who qualifies for them, regardless of income. Two main examples in the UK of such benefits are the state pension and **child benefit.** Clearly, these benefits do not target those on low incomes, but they do ensure that everyone in the relevant categories does receive the benefit.

KEY WORDS

Government intervention	Discounting technique (to compare future costs and benefits)
Taxes	
Subsidies	
Indirect tax	Benefit-cost ratios
Internalisation of an externality	Price controls
Environmental damage	Minimum price
Road charges	Maximum price
Road tolls	Surplus
Free provision	Minimum wage
Economies of scale	Unemployment
Regional policies	Privatised monopolies
Training of labour	Monopoly practices
Redistribution of income	Price-fixing
Tax incentives	OFTEL
Interest free loans	Legal controls
Carbon reduction targets	Infrastructure
Government provision	Good faith
Universally used services	Information provision
Cost-benefit analysis	Progressive tax
Economic welfare	Lorenz curve
Net social benefit	Cash benefits
Monetary value (of externalities)	Means-tested benefits
Value of a human life	Universal benefits
Principle of 'willingness to pay'	Child benefit

Conclusion

The perceived problems of the free market outlined in chapters 4 and 5 imply that there is a case for government intervention in the running of the economy. There is a range of different policies that can be and are employed to overcome the problems. Unfortunately, as outlined in chapter 7, when the government intervenes to try to overcome market failures and concerns over inequity it can sometimes make the situation worse rather than better.

Further reading

Atkinson, B. *et al.*, Chapter 19 in *Applied Economics*, Macmillan, 1998.

Burningham, D and Davies, J., Chapter 6 in *Green Economics*, 2nd edn, Heinemann, 1999.

Lipsey, R. and Chrystal, A., Chapter 19 in *Principles of Economics*, Oxford University Press, 9th edn, 1999.

Sloman, J., Chapter 11 in *Economics*, Prentice Hall, 4th edn, 2000.

Useful websites

The Guardian: www.newsunlimited.co.uk/
The Independent: www.independent.co.uk/
The Daily Telegraph: www.telegraph.co.uk/
The Times: www.the-times.co.uk/
Advertising Standards Authority: www.asa.org.uk/

Essay topics

1. (a) Using examples, distinguish between:
   (i) a private good and a public good, and
   (ii) a positive externality and a negative externality.   [10 marks]
   (b) Examine how and why a government might provide public goods and reduce negative externalities.   [15 marks]
   [OCR, November 1995]
2. (a) Distinguish, with the aid of examples, between positive and negative externalities.   [10 marks]
   (b) Discuss the extent to which subsidies to producers are the best means for a government to encourage the consumption of goods and services that generate positive externalities.   [15 marks]
   [OCR, March 1996]

Data response question

This task is based on a question set by the OCR exam board in 2000. Study the passage and the figure below and then answer the questions that follow.

The problem of pollution

Every day, there are innumerable instances where firms and other organisations pollute their local environment, deliberately in the main but sometimes by accident. The extract below, taken from a national newspaper, reports on a particular case whereby the polluter was successfully prosecuted for the environmental problems caused by a spillage of chemicals into a local river.

Water firm is fined over salmon deaths

A water company was fined £175,000 yesterday for poisoning a salmon river. Severn Trent Water admitted leaking chemicals into the Wye, killing 33,000 young salmon – 98 per cent of the stock in the river.

Cardiff Crown Court heard that the leak was the company's 34th conviction since privatisation in 1990. Judge John Prosser criticised the company for its poor record and described its management as 'very slack indeed'. Mark Bailey, prosecuting for the National Rivers Authority, said that pollution from the Elan Valley water treatment works, at Rhayader, Powys, had 'catastrophic consequences for the river'.

'An estimated 33,000 young salmon were exterminated by this leak, which affected eight kilometres of river',, he said. 'It is relatively easy to replace adult salmon, but these young salmon need to be replaced with the fish from the same gene pool. Severn Trent caused this catastrophe through a collection of errors, including bad management and inferior maintenance. The area is one of the most significant salmon fishing areas in England and Wales and this is one of the most significant incidents. The sheer number of fish killed is higher than any other incident.'

Judge Prosser told water company executives sitting in the court that the leak was due to design defects, gross mismanagement and inferior maintenance. The company also claimed it was not responsible for the whole of the pollution.

Incidents such as the one described above are the outcome of a situation whereby the market mechanism has failed to produce the best allocation of resources due to negative externalities. Economists can explain the pollution of the River Wye by Severn Trent Water in terms of the diagram shown in Figure A on the following page.

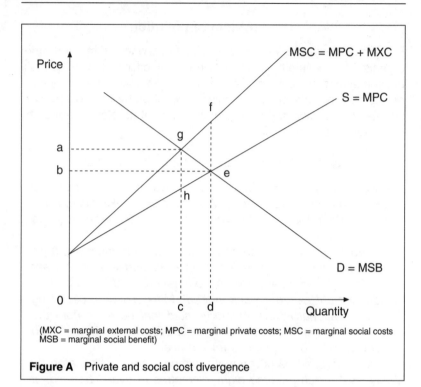

(MXC = marginal external costs; MPC = marginal private costs; MSC = marginal social costs
MSB = marginal social benefit)

Figure A Private and social cost divergence

Source: Adapted from Wilkinson, M., *Equity, Efficiency and Market Failure*, Heinemann, 1997 and *The Daily Telegraph*, 6 August 1996

1. (a) Describe what is meant by a negative externality.

    [2 marks]

    (b) Use the evidence in the newspaper article to show how negative externalities apply to this particular pollution incident.

    [6 marks]

2. Use Figure A to answer the following questions and, in each case, assume a competitive market operates with no government intervention.

    (a) What would be the market equilibrium price and output? Explain your answer. [4 marks]

    (b) What would be the price and output at the social optimum? Explain your answer. [4 marks]

    (c) What are the consequences for the firm and for its consumers of the differences between price and output levels at the market equilibrium and the social optimum? [6 marks]

3. (a) Drawing upon the case described in the newspaper article, state the arguments for and against fines as a means of reducing environmental pollution. [6 marks]

   (b) With the help of Figure A, explain how it might be possible to apply a pollution charge or green tax in this particular case. [7 marks]

4. Suppose the National Rivers Authority decides to consider closing the present Elan Valley water treatment works and recommend its replacement with a new works in a different site. Discuss how an economist might use the cost-benefit approach to determine whether this action should be taken. [10 marks]

Chapter Seven

Government failure

'Most of the energy of political work is devoted to correcting the effects of the mismanagement of government.'
Milton Friedman

'Giving money and power to government is like giving whiskey and keys to teenage boys.'
P.J. O'Rourke

The suggestion of chapter 6 was that governments could legitimately intervene in the functioning of markets in order to improve the level of economic efficiency. Where market failures were present, it was indicated that the appropriate government intervention could help correct those failures and thus lead to a better use of scarce resources than if things were left to the market. Unfortunately, there may be more to the story than this. Governments, as well as markets, may fail.

Government failure *exists when government intervention in markets leads to economic inefficiency.* It can be seen that there are reasons why government attempts to introduce policies correcting market failures may themselves create further inefficiencies. The reasons for this can be divided into three main problems:

1. **Problems of information.**
2. **Problems of incentives.**
3. **Problems of distribution.**

Information problems
Once the government starts to intervene in the running of markets, it requires information. The appropriate policies can only be introduced if the appropriate information is possessed by the government. This was not true with the free market. As long as people knew what they wanted and were prepared to pay for it, then free markets could be seen to function to produce the products that consumers demanded. This was seen as one of the great strengths of the market in chapter 3: there was no need for anybody to have to use a great deal of scarce resources gathering information in order to make economic decisions.

There are various sorts of information that are required by the government in order to ensure that its intervention to correct market failures is appropriate:

- *What is the appropriate level of tax to set when correcting a negative externality?* If production of a good generating negative externalities is to be moved to the appropriate level, then the exact value of that external cost will have to be known. This will allow an appropriate tax rate to be set. However, this is a difficult calculation. The article in chapter 6 about the problems of setting the right road charge in Leicester indicates the problem (see page 65).
- *What level of subsidy is required?* A similar problem exists with subsidies for merit goods and products generating positive externalities. The precise value of the positive externality must be known if the right subsidy is to be given to producers.
- *What is the right maximum price?* If a maximum price is introduced to try to control the behaviour of monopolies, then information about what might be the price if the market were competitive will have to be gathered. This may be very difficult when there are no direct comparisons.
- *What is the right minimum price?* What level should a minimum wage be to protect low earners but not to create (significant) unemployment?
- *How much of a public good should the government provide?* The problem with the decision to intervene to provide a good or service is that information must then be found to work out how much to produce. The free market would work this out by consumers registering their desires in the market place. The government must work out other ways of gathering the appropriate information. This could prove to be very difficult, especially if people see an incentive to state too little preference (because they have to pay) or too much preference (because someone else's taxes pay for them). The problems of cost-benefit analysis considered in chapter 6 indicate some of the information problems involved.

There are two problems that can then arise due to these demands for information for successful government intervention:

1. *The government may get the calculation wrong.* Given the difficulties involved in gaining the information, there is every chance that wrong or inadequate information may be used and thus that the wrong policy is introduced. A tax or a subsidy may be set at too high or too low a level. This will mean that allocative

efficiency is not restored in the market and there is no guarantee that the level of production is any more economically desirable than before the government intervention.

2. *Gathering the information incurs a cost.* Time and effort required to gather the information required to try to make the appropriate policy decisions has a cost in terms of scarce resources. There is thus an opportunity cost as alternative uses for these resources (making products that could have given consumer satisfaction) cannot take place. This can soon be seen as economic inefficiency: scarce resources are not being used directly to meet infinite wants and thus may not be being used in the best possible way. The level of this cost is often seen as becoming excessive and unnecessary: hence the terms **'bureaucracy'** and **'red tape'**.

Problems with incentives

Further problems can be seen to arise when government intervention takes place because there may be undesirable effects on incentives due to such intervention. These can be seen in three particular areas:

1. The distortion of incentives due to the introduction of taxes and benefits.
2. The motivation of politicians.
3. The incentives of those running government services.

Incentives and taxes and benefits

Various forms of government intervention require finance. Obvious examples include the government provision of public goods and the payment of cash benefits. The necessary finance is raised by the government through the tax system: taxes are imposed on producers and consumers so that defence, education and health care can be provided and benefits paid to different groups and individuals. This sounds a simple solution, but the problem is that such taxes are likely to affect people's incentives in a way that may reduce economic efficiency as resources are used less effectively.

The most obvious example of incentives being affected is the **incentive to work**. A tax on people's income (or equally upon their spent income or expenditure) will have an impact upon the incentive to work. The overall impact may in fact be complicated, but there is clearly a possibility that the imposition of a tax by a government on people's income may lead people to think that working is now less worthwhile and thus they may work less. This would lead to labour being less productive and a scarce resource not being used to its full potential. There would not be economic efficiency.

The same problem of the undesirable distortion of incentives can be seen with an expenditure tax. This is shown in Figure 17 where the imposition of a **flat-rate expenditure tax** of 't' causes the supply schedule to move to the left (S to S_1). This leads to a lower quantity and a higher price. The problem is that an area of both **producer surplus** and **consumer surplus** is lost due to this lower level of production and consumption. Desirable trades have been discouraged and thus some economic welfare has been lost: there is a move away from Pareto efficiency. The amount of this is shown by the area 'abc'. In economics, it is referred to as the **'deadweight loss'** of a tax.

If taxes can be seen as creating undesirable incentives, then similar problems can be caused by benefits that are paid to people due to concerns about the distribution of income in society. Paying people who are unemployed to help them not to suffer unacceptable poverty may reduce the incentive for unemployed people to find employment. Scarce resources may thus not be used. A similar sort of undesirable effect on incentives can be seen in the article below about the student forced to leave school. Government intervention to address problems with the market can be seen as creating further inefficiencies, in this case the lack of development of an important factor of production.

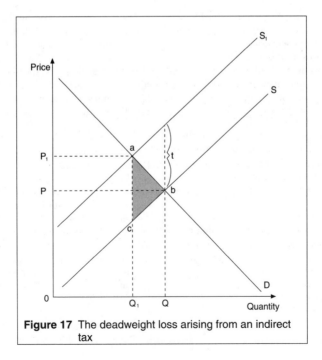

Figure 17 The deadweight loss arising from an indirect tax

The motivation of politicians

Decisions regarding economic intervention in the running of markets are taken by politicians who are elected to run a country. This is the democratic system. However, this creates a potential problem with the economic policy process that could lead to inefficiency.

The problem with politicians is that there are perfectly under-standable reasons why their sole motivation may not be to judge the desirability of an economic policy purely in terms of its impact on economic efficiency. They have a clear interest in securing their political future. Specifically, that means ensuring that they gain re-election at the appropriate time. Their aim can be seen as trying

Benefits trap forces sixth-former with hopes of university to leave school

Liz Lightfoot

Lauren Dewart has worked hard in the sixth form of Torquay Girls' Grammar school and is holding an offer to study medicine at university.

But this week she will be forced to leave school and abandon her college hopes because of legislation affecting pupils who turn 19.

Though the government is keen to encourage pupils to stay on at school, there is no financial support for sixth-formers. Parents who are unemployed or on low incomes can claim benefits for dependent children, but only to the age of 18.

From her birthday on December 30 Lauren will be classed as an adult by the benefits system and her unemployed mother will no longer be given money to keep her. Lauren will not be able to claim because she is at school and not available for work.

The Education Department, however, considers her a child, which means she cannot take out a student loan. Nor can she claim access grants available to students at further education colleges. Instead, Patricia Dewart, a single mother from Torquay, Devon, will have to keep herself and Lauren on a single person's £51.40 a week. Mother and daughter will also have to move out of their £92-a-week two-bedroom flat when Mrs Dewart's housing benefit is cut from £80 to £40.

Lauren, who works on Friday evenings and on Saturdays in a super-market to supplement the family income, is expected to get three 'A's at 'A'-level.

'All I am asking for is a loan to tide me over the next eight months until I start university and qualify for a student loan,' she said.

The Daily Telegraph, 13 December 1999

to maximise votes. This incentive may over-rule the most desirable economic course of action and lead to a less than optimum use of scarce resources.

This possibility was mentioned in chapter 6 in the article about cost-benefit analyses of proposed road schemes (see page 72). Two of those accepted were seen to be in areas where there could be political gain in a desired new road scheme being built. Resources could have been better used in other areas, but the political gain would not be so great.

The motivation of public employees

It is not only politicians whose motivations may not be in line with what is best for achieving economic efficiency. People working for government-run organisations may also have uncertain incentives.

In the free market, the profit motive is seen as driving forward entrepreneurs. The desire for this personal gain was seen in chapter 3 as leading to the products that consumers wanted being produced at the lowest possible cost. There is no obvious similar motivation at work in government organisations. What incentives are there for the right products to be produced at the lowest possible cost? A motivation of public service would be ideal, but economics tends to assume that the strongest motivation is for personal gain and satisfaction. If that is so, then those in charge of public services may not seek to ensure that costs are as low as they can be and that the very best possible service is provided to all consumers. An easy life with the highest possible salary would clearly be possible alternative motivations. If that were the case, then scarce resources would not be seen to be used in the most effective way possible.

This was often seen as the problem of nationalised industries owned and run by the government. A lack of appropriate incentives appeared to lead to high levels of inefficiency and thus the need to privatise these industries in an effort to introduce more market-based incentives.

This problem might explain the problem of public sector fraud reported in the article below from *The Independent*. The incentive to make money in fraudulent ways from the public services clearly can be greater than the desire to ensure the provision of an efficient service. This certainly implies an inappropriate use of scarce resources.

Distribution problems

A further difficulty may occur through governments intervening in the functioning of markets because such intervention will always have some impact upon the distribution of wealth and income.

Public sector fraud is costing Britain £108m

PAUL WAUGH

Fraud in town halls and the NHS has risen to record levels, with greater numbers of GPs, opticians and pharmacists attempting to fiddle the system, according to figures published by the Audit Commission today.

Fraud amounting to more than £108m was uncovered in the past year. Councils in England and Wales detected £104m in illegal payments, up 18 per cent on 1997–98, while fraud in the NHS doubled to £4.7m. For the first time corrupt GPs have been highlighted in the statistics, with more doctors than ever making false claims for prescriptions, vaccinations and night visits. The figures relate only to fraud which has been identified as having occurred; the suspected amount of undiscovered fraud is far higher.

Abuse of the system

GPs: Husband and wife GPs claimed back from the NHS the cost of drugs for bogus vaccinations and contraceptive services. Theft of £45,000 uncovered after they fled the country.

Opticians: An optician made claims exceeding all the other practices in the area – £200,000 of suspect claims in three years.

Pharmacists: A pharmacist with two shops collected prescription fees but, where drugs cost less than the fee, pocketed the cash. Claimed £42,000 by pretending one shop was ordering from the other.

Council officers: A woman officer who banked town hall's income from parking fines stole the cash element and banked only cheques. She took a total of £110,000. A manager in a housing benefit section of a council set up 13 fictitious landlords and submitted claims from their non-existent tenants. More than £431,000 was stolen.

The Independent, 1 December 1999

At times, the government intervention may be a deliberate attempt to improve what is seen as an inequitable distribution. However, any use of taxes, subsidies, benefits, government provision of goods and services and maximum and minimum prices will have a different impact upon different individuals and groups within society. As such, it will change the distribution of wealth and income. At the very least, this complicates the decision about the appropriate form of government intervention to use. It could even lead to a policy that appears desirable on grounds of economic efficiency being deemed undesirable because of its distributional effect.

A clear example of this problem was seen in the 1990s with John Major's Conservative government's attempt to introduce VAT at the standard rate of 17.5 per cent on domestic fuel and power. Such a policy could certainly have been justified on grounds of economic efficiency. The use of domestic fuel could be seen as contributing to the generation of the negative externalities associated with global warming (see chapter 8). It might also be deemed as a scarce resource in danger of over-use. As such, a tax could be justified (especially as most other products were already taxed at such a rate). However, the problem was that certain sections of society would clearly be hit harder than others by such a tax: it would have a clear distributional impact. Specifically, poorer pensioners who spent a significant amount of their budget on domestic fuel and power would be hit the hardest. This was deemed to be inequitable and the final result was that the move to introduce VAT at 17.5 per cent was defeated. (It was finally introduced at a rate of 8 per cent and then further reduced to 5 per cent.) The article below from *The Daily Telegraph* announcing this also makes plain again how political considerations can over-ride possible arguments about economic efficiency.

Major defeated by Tory revolt over VAT rise

GEORGE JONES

The Government was defeated over VAT on domestic fuel and power last night when MPs voted by 319 votes to 311, a majority of eight, against increasing the tax to 17.5 per cent next April. It was the biggest blow to the Government's authority since Mr John Major became Prime Minister and will force Mr Kenneth Clarke, the Chancellor, to rewrite last week's budget.

Tory rebels joined forces with Labour and other Opposition parties to demand a rethink on the decision to double VAT on gas and electricity bills.

In the closing moments of five tense days of debate on the Budget, and to loud Opposition jeers, Mr Clarke first offered a further £20 million to help people with insulation through the home energy efficiency programme.

Then, to further jeers, he agreed to meet the demands of a principal Tory rebel and leading campaigner for pensioners, Sir Andrew Bowden, to uprate the compensation for pensioners.

After a day of meetings with Tory opponents of VAT, Mr Clarke promised that a single pensioner would receive another 50p a week next April and a married couple 70p to help meet the increased cost of their fuel bills.

But most of the rebels were not persuaded. They regarded VAT on fuel as an unpopular tax – rivalling the poll tax – and wanted to prevent it going ahead.

The Daily Telegraph, 7 December 1994

It could be argued that this incident highlights a further difficulty with governments intervening in markets, namely the difficulties of the legislative process required to put the policy in place. Any government economic policy has to go through considerable legislative procedures before it can become law. At the very least, this can mean that any desired policy is delayed.

Conclusion

The message of this chapter is that governments can fail as well as markets. A market failure can lead to legitimate government intervention in the operation of the market. In principle, this can improve the level of economic efficiency in that market. However, because of the problems considered in this chapter, there is no guarantee that economic efficiency will improve due to government intervention. There is a possibility that there will be greater economic inefficiency than before the intervention occurred.

KEY WORDS

Government failure	Producer surplus
Information problems	Incentive to work
Incentive problems	Flat-rate expenditure tax
Distributional problems	Consumer surplus
Bureaucracy	Deadweight loss
Red tape	

Further reading

Grant, S., Chapters 25 and 62 in Stanlake's *Introductory Economics*, 7th edn., Longman, 2000.

Lipsey, R. and Chrystal, A., Chapter 19 in *Principles of Economics*, Oxford University Press, 9th edn, 1999.

Munday, S., Chapter 13 in *Current Developments in Economics*, Macmillan, 1996.

Sloman, J., Chapter 11 in *Economics*, Prentice Hall, 4th edn, 2000.

Useful websites

The *Financial Times*: www.ft.com/

National Institute of Economic and Social Research: www.niesr.ac.uk/

The Treasury: www.hm-treasury.gov.uk/

Essay topics
1. Distinguish between public, private and merit goods. [10 marks]
2. With reference to public, private and merit goods, on what grounds, if at all, should there be subsidies for libraries?
[OCR, November 1998]   [15 marks]
3. In 1997 the EU proposed a ban on all cigarette advertising and sponsorship of sporting and arts events.
(a) Why might the EU wish to impose such a ban?   [30 marks]
(b) How might tobacco companies react to the ban?   [30 marks]
(c) Evaluate two alternate policies which governments might adopt to reduce tobacco consumption   [40 marks]
[Edexcel, June 1999]

Data response question
This task is based on a question set by the OCR exam board for its Markets specimen paper for 2000. Study the passage, graph and table, and then answer the questions that follow.

Townley Regional Health Authority

All of us at some time in our lives require the services of doctors, dentists and hospitals. Traditionally, in the UK, these services have been provided by the public sector, free of charge to users. Like any sector of the economy though, there is a genuine problem of how to meet the health care needs of the community from the limited resources available. The problem of health care is a very good illustration of what economists mean by the 'economic problem'.

The task of allocating resources for health care is carried out by organisations known as Regional Health Authorities. Due to the nature of their funding, there is a maximum quantity of health care that can be provided at any one time. The regional health authority in Townley is faced with just such a problem.

Suppose it has to provide just two services to the community, medical services through local doctors (GPs) and dental services through local dental practices. The Production Possibility Frontier in Figure A shows some of the trade-offs facing the Townley Regional Health Authority.

Due to financial pressures and increased demands for its services, the Townley Regional Health Authority is continuously seeking to make a more effective use of its resources.

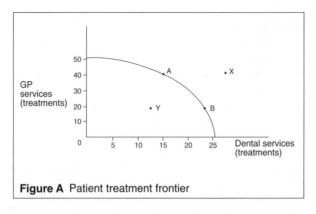

Figure A Patient treatment frontier

The Molar Dental Practice, like other dentists in Townley, has recently taken the decision to 'opt out' of the control of the Townley Regional Health Authority. It is now one of a large and growing number of private dental practices in the town which treat only private patients who pay the 'full cost' for any treatment they receive. Market research undertaken for the practice shows the estimated demand schedule for the services it provides. This information is shown in Table A below.

Other private dentists in Townley do not charge exactly the same price for treatment as the Molar Dental Practice. However, the market is a very competitive one, with businesses seeking to enhance their reputation in order to attract new patients who are seeking private dental treatment. At present, all private dentists are in a situation where they are able to take on any new patients who are willing to pay the charge for the treatment they receive.

Table A Estimated demand schedule for treatment provided by the Molar Dental Practice

Average price of treatment	Quantity of treatment demanded per month
40	350
35	375
30	400
25	450
20	500
15	600
10	800

1. (a) Define the term 'opportunity cost'. [2 marks]
   (b) With reference to Figure A, explain the trade-offs which are facing the Townley Regional Health Authority. [4 marks]
   (c) How can opportunity cost be used to explain the shape of the production possibility frontier? [2 marks]
   (d) If the Townley Regional Health Authority makes a more effective use of its resources, how will this affect the production possibility frontier? [2 marks]
2. (a) Use the data in the table to sketch the demand curve for services of the Molar Dental Practice and explain the shape of this curve. [4 marks]
   (b) If the income level of patients falls, use a diagram to explain how this might affect the demand for dental services provided by Molar Dental Practice. [4 marks]
3. The 'full cost' of providing dental services consists of some costs which are fixed and other costs which are variable.
   (a) With aid of examples, explain the difference between fixed and variable costs for the Molar Dental Practice. [4 marks]
   (b) If the wages of dental nurses increase, how might this affect the prices charged by the Molar Dental Practice to its patients? [5 marks]
4. With reference to the data shown in Table A,
   (a) Briefly explain how this data might have been collected. [5 marks]
   (b) Comment upon its usefulness to the owners of the Molar Dental Practice. [5 marks]
5. An economist would argue that the market for private dental treatment in Townley is an example of monopolistic competition. Using the evidence in the last two paragraphs, discuss the extent to which this market is an example of monopolistic competition. [8 marks]

Chapter Eight

The environment

'Our new data and understanding now point to the critical situation we face: to slow future change, we must start taking action now . . . Ignoring climate change will surely be the most costly of all possible choices, for us and for our children.'
Peter D. Ewins (Chief Executive Officer, UK Meteorological Office) and D. James Baker (Under Secretary, US National Oceanic and Atmospheric Administration) (1999)

All of us feel some concern about the environment. We know that there is damage occurring although we are perhaps unsure quite how serious it is and how soon undesirable consequences will occur. We probably know that 'something needs to be done' but are unsure of both what is really possible and desirable.

For the economist, the problem over the environment is an economic one. Our environment is clearly a vital scarce resource and there is concern that it is not being used in the optimum way. To use the language of this book, there seems to be economic inefficiency. In turn, this suggests that there is market failure and thus that there might be some appropriate corrective action that governments can take to improve economic efficiency. The aim of this chapter is thus two-fold:

1. To understand the environmental problem in terms of the appropriate economic theory.
2. To suggest possible government economic policies that might help to lead to a better use of the relevant scarce resources.

The environmental problem
There are two key examples of market failures that can help us to understand the environmental problem:

- Negative externalities.
- Public and quasi-public goods.

Negative externalities
One way of understanding the problem of environmental damage and pollution is to see it as an example of a negative externality, as explained in chapter 4. The essence of the problem is that all

environmental damage and pollution clearly creates a significant social cost but this is not represented in the private cost to producers and consumers. This means that there is an external cost (or negative externality) that in turn implies that there is an over-production of those products that generate environmental damage and pollution. This is as illustrated in Figure 8 in chapter 4.

Environmental damage as an example of a negative externality is clearly seen with the concerns over **global warming**. Global warming is seen to occur due to the so-called 'greenhouse effect'. This is caused by the accumulation of certain **gases** that allow the sun's radiation into the earth's atmosphere but then prevent the escape of some of that radiation. Thus, the earth becomes warmer over a period of time. Current human activities, such as the burning of **fossil fuels**, are increasing the concentration of these gases, notably carbon dioxide (one of the four main gases involved). Two main possible consequences of this effect have been identified:

1. Agricultural effects. Those with warm climates are likely to suffer (negative externalities) as temperatures rise. Those with colder climates may benefit (positive externalities) as temperatures rise.
2. Rising sea levels. The predicted rise of sea levels of 66 centimetres by 2100 would cause the negative externalities of increased flooding and land loss.

Those burning fossil fuels take account of the private financial cost of purchasing the fuel. They do not take account of the possible costs to agriculture and land loss. Third parties are affected and there is a negative externality.

There are two further important points to note about the nature of environmental damage as negative externalities:

1. The spill-over **effects are global.** The third parties that are affected by the actions of others are not just in the country of origin of the source of the environmental damage: they are throughout the world. This is quite clearly true with global warming but is certainly the case with other environmental concerns such as damage to the ozone layer and acid rain. This implies any government policy will have to be global in nature.
2. The spill-over effects are often relevant for future generations. It is not just third parties today who are affected by environmental damage. The main consequences may well be felt by third parties in future generations. This raises a difficult question about how such costs should be valued in any consideration of the right policy

to be implemented today. Should possible future costs be given the same value as costs today? Or should such future costs be discounted so that they represent a lower value than any current costs? That important value judgement will have an impact on current government intervention.

Public and quasi-public goods

The economic concepts of public and quasi-public goods further help our understanding of the environmental problem. It can be suggested that the essence of the problem with the environment is that it is not a pure public good but is rather a quasi-public good. If it were a pure public good, there would be no environmental problem. Unfortunately it is not. Specifically, it can be seen that the environment appears to possess the characteristic of non-excludability but not of non-rivalry. People are not or cannot be stopped from making use of the resource of the environment. However, there is certainly a point after which the environment is rival. As more and more use of it is made in different ways by more and more people, then so the benefit to everyone of its use is diminished.

It is helpful to consider where different aspects of the environment as a product may sit on the spectrum between pure public goods and pure private goods. This has to be done by considering both properties of excludability and rivalry. With regard to rivalry, three categories can be identified:

- Non-rival. Any amount of consumers does not diminish the benefit to others.
- Congestible. Up to a point, new consumers do not affect the benefit of others. However, after a certain point, benefit starts to diminish for all as new consumers arrive.
- Rival. Any extra consumer will always diminish the benefit to those already consuming.

With this in mind, the following grid can be devised:

	Non-exclusive	Exclusive
Non-rival	Pure public good Nuclear defence system	Intellectual property Literature
Congestible	Air supply Atmosphere	Private swimming-pool Private garden
Rival	Fishery Common grazing land	Pure private good Many consumer goods

Environmental products appear to fall either into the category of non-exclusive and congestible or non-exclusive and rival. Global warming appears to suggest that once a certain amount of greenhouse gases are emitted into the atmosphere, then there is an effect of global warming that may have undesirable consequences. There will be an over-use of the atmosphere in the free market.

There will also be an over-use of grazing land and fisheries in the free market. Consider a goat-herder who finds an area of pasture that his goat can use free of charge. This allows his goat to put on 15 kilos in weight, a beneficial course of action for the goat-herder to take. However, if other goats are already grazing this land, it is possible that this weight gain is made at the expense of all other goats gaining 15 kilos less in weight in total. Thus, there is no net social benefit. Such land can quickly become over-grazed.

The work of R. Coase (1960) can also be seen in terms of the above grid. Coase suggested that the problem of externalities is that there is a lack of **property rights**. In other words, some things are not owned by anyone. This is true with some environmental products such as the atmosphere and the air supply. It is this lack of ownership that means that the products are non-excludable. If someone or some people owned the atmosphere, then access could be restricted and the product would be excludable. Thus, it might not be over-used. Lack of ownership explains environmental damage.

Government policies to tackle the environmental problem

There are many possible government policies that have and could be used to try to tackle the environmental problem. Four types of policies are considered here:

1. **Environmental taxation.**
2. **Marketable permits.**
3. Property rights systems.
4. **Regulation.**

Environmental taxation

The standard response to an externality was seen in chapter 6 to be to try to internalise that externality: force the relevant producer or consumer to pay the true social cost associated with the production and consumption of the product. The clearest way of doing this with a negative externality is to impose a tax. The effect of this was illustrated in Figure 13 in chapter 6.

The key thing with regard to environmental damage is to isolate

Conservation lobby happy as Brown goes green

CHARLES CLOVER

Labour's first 'green' tax, a levy on the business use of energy, was announced by the Chancellor yesterday along with a large package of environmental tax reforms which were welcomed by conservationists.

Michael Meacher, the environment minister, claimed that it was 'the greenest budget we've ever had' and Patricia Hewitt, the economic secretary, described it as 'the largest and most radical package of environmental tax reforms ever announced in this country'.

The business energy tax is expected to raise £1.75 billion a year from April 2001. The tax will discourage energy use but is supposed not to damage competitiveness. It will be returned to business in the form of a reduction in employers' national insurance contributions.

The tax – likely to be levied at a rate of 0.6p per kilowatt hour for electricity – will save 1.5 million tons of carbon dioxide a year and contribute to Britain's legally-binding target, set in Kyoto, of reducing 12.5 per cent of all greenhouse gases by 2010.

Conservationists welcomed the tax and the rest of the environmental package, which included the introduction of a £1 a year rise in the landfill tax which reaches £10 a year in April; the end of tax breaks for excessive mileage in company cars and a £55 cut in vehicle excise duty for small cars. New cars will be taxed from 2002 on the amount of carbon dioxide they emit and the price of ultra-low sulphur diesel will be reduced by a further 1p.

Friends of the Earth said that the budget showed Labour had taken 'its first halting steps towards **green economics**' and gave the Chancellor six out of 10 for effort. There will also be measures designed to encourage green commuting.

The Daily Telegraph, 10 March 1999

the product that is responsible for the damage. This is not always easy as there may be several products and the precise effect of each is not known. With the example of global warming, it has been suggested that a relevant tax might be a '**carbon tax**'. Each of the three fossil fuels, coal, oil and gas, could be taxed according to their carbon content. It is the carbon content of these fuels that is responsible for emissions of carbon dioxide, one of the key greenhouse gases responsible for global warming. Thus, the negative externality has to be paid for: it is internalised.

The article about recent environmental taxes indicates the sort of taxes that can be introduced to try to internalise the external environmental costs of fuel use as well as other measures to help the environment.

Chapter 7 pointed out that there are often problems whenever the government makes the decision to intervene in the market. This is true with an environmental tax. Two particular issues are as follows:

1. *Setting the tax at the appropriate level.* It is very hard to calculate the level of negative externality attributable to different products. It is thus very difficult to set the 'correct' tax rate.
2. *Co-ordinating policy between countries.* The problem with much environmental damage is that it is a world-wide issue. This implies the need for a world-wide response. If the UK sets a high carbon tax, then companies may simply move to another country with a lower carbon tax. The overall levels of carbon dioxide emissions may not be reduced.

Marketable permits

A different approach to controlling aspects of the environmental problem is to issue marketable permits to companies that allow them to pollute the atmosphere (for example with carbon dioxide emissions) by a certain amount. These permits can then be traded. If more than the specified amount of emissions is sought by the company, then it will have to purchase the permits from other companies. If less than the permitted level of emissions is sought by the company, then it can sell some of its emissions rights to other companies.

This system allows a certain target level of pollution (potentially on a global scale) to be agreed and then allows the market in the issued permits to create appropriate incentives and force companies responsible for high emissions to pay high costs as they have to purchase permits from others. The external cost becomes a private cost.

This raises an important question as to how the appropriate level of pollution might be discovered. The suggestion of economic theory is that this will not be zero. An optimum amount of pollution can be discovered by comparing the **damage costs** of pollution with the **costs of pollution reduction**. There will be an **optimum level of pollution** (such as carbon dioxide emissions) where the combination of these two costs is minimised. This is illustrated in Figure 18 where the optimum level of carbon dioxide emissions is at C_1 as at this point the damage costs added to the costs of reducing the emissions are at their lowest point. This then could give the target total level of carbon dioxide emissions for the world and permits to emit carbon dioxide could be given out to different countries totalling this amount.

The article below about emissions trading indicates that this policy may be a positive way forward in moving towards a more optimal use of the scarce resource of our environment.

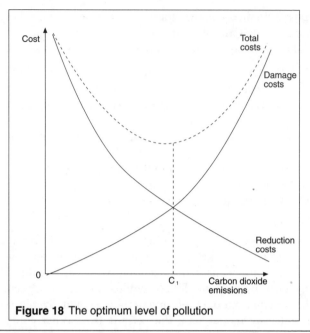

Figure 18 The optimum level of pollution

Report shows international emissions trading can reduce the costs of climate change

A new report released today by the Pew Center on Global Climate Change highlights the importance of international emissions trading in reducing the costs of climate change. An international greenhouse gas emissions trading regime would significantly lower global mitigation costs, the report states.

'As policy-makers explore ways to meet the global challenge of climate change, emissions trading should be high on their agenda', said Eileen Claussen, President of the Pew Center on Global Climate Change. 'Greenhouse gases released anywhere in the world can contribute to changes in global temperatures. In international emissions trading capitalizes on this by allowing the lowest costs emissions reductions to occur first'.

While broader participation in trading is likely to yield greater benefits, any amount of trading will lower the costs of those participating, the report states.

'International trade holds the potential of reducing costs of controlling world emissions of greenhouse gases because the nations of the world experience very different costs for achieving emissions reductions on their own', Claussen said.

PR Newswire, Washington, 14 December 1999

Property rights systems

The approach to negative externalities used by Coase would suggest that the key to ensuring the proper use of the environment is to ensure that it is owned. If it is clearly the property of certain identifiable people, then the owners can:

- charge anyone who wishes to damage the environment in any way
- sue those who damage the environment without the permission of the owners.

Thus the external cost is put on to those responsible for it. The externality is internalised.

Such an approach was suggested in the United Kingdom in a Green Paper published in March, 1993. The idea was that the level of damage caused by something such as the dumping of toxic waste should be determined and then awards made by the judicial system. However, there are problems with such a system:

- Property rights have to be negotiated. Who should be given ownership rights to the environment?
- Legal costs can be high. This may imply that it is not worth suing the perpetrator of environmental damage.
- The problem of **synergism**. This means that it is very difficult to trace the exact cause and effect of any environmental damage attributable to any one party given the number of possible contributors.

Regulation

Economists tend not to see regulation as an ideal policy. It does not work with the market but rather directly against it. A policy such as taxation tries to nudge and encourage the market in a certain direction while still allowing it to function. However, regulation over-rules the market entirely. A policy to make various forms of pollution illegal simply outlaws the possibility: it removes consumer and producer choice. In general, such a policy might be likely to lead to further misuse of resources and thus create government failure.

However, there are examples where there is no obvious way of allowing the market to function effectively. The provision of public goods was seen as an example of this in chapters 4 and 6. There could be examples with environmental issues. Coase's suggestion was that ownership rights should be given and that this was a means of restricting access to environmental products that were previously non-excludable. However, it may be that giving such clear ownership

Fishy business

The latest swingeing cuts in European fishing quotas are both sensible and dismaying. They make sense, because we know that fish stocks, drastically depleted by generations of greed and stupidity, urgently need to be protected. They are dismaying, because they will bring hardship and anger to the practitioners of an ancient coastal tradition. And for those of us who adore eating fresh fish, they are an alarming harbinger of sharply rising prices.

The fishermen are understandably angry that new limits are being imposed on their livelihood. But we must be wary of their claim that they are themselves the best judges of conservation needs and techniques. Where there is good money to be made by trawling the sea to exhaustion, particularly in another nation's waters, then some are always willing to do it.

The central facts are surely indisputable. 'Improved' methods of factory fishing have devastated the oceans. Shoals of fish can be precisely located, and efficiently scooped from the water.

The quota system is imperfect in a number of ways. If a fishing vessel inadvertently or carelessly goes over quota, the surplus is casually destroyed and lost forever. Those who have leeway to make up use ever more desperate and dubious techniques to achieve their targets. But it is an imperfect world, and quotas are probably the best method on offer to conserve our dwindling stocks.

News Unlimited, 17 December 1999

rights to one person or group of people is not deemed to be possible. Too many parties have a legitimate claim to the product and its use. In that case, regulation may be required to try to restrict access and prevent over-use.

An example of such regulation to attempt to restrict access is the use of fishing quotas to prevent over-fishing of fisheries. Rather than saying that one person or government is the sole owner of a particular sea (such as The Channel) which could be politically impossible, **quotas** are issued restricting how much fish can be caught. The article about this suggests how such quotas are bound to be unpopular but it is clear that this market will continue to fail disastrously without such intervention. The alternative appears to be the end of our stocks of fish.

Conclusion

Economic theory provides a framework that enables us to understand environmental problems. Clear market failures can be identified that seem to be leading to the misuse of the scarce resource of the environment. This implies the potential desirability of government intervention in an effort to lead to a better use of environmental resources and lead to greater economic efficiency. However, designing appropriate policies is very difficult, especially in the face of some of the specific difficulties in this area such as:

- the global nature of the problem
- the uncertainty about the precise effects
- the fact that most of the costs are likely to be borne by future generations.

Governments are bound to fail in their attempts. However, the size of the market failure that is now perceived and the scale of the misuse of resources suggest that even with some government failure, government intervention is seen as a necessity.

KEY WORDS

Global warming	Optimum level of pollution
Greenhouse effect	Carbon tax
Greenhouse gases	Regulation
Fossil fuels	Green economics
Global effects	Damage costs
Congestible	Pollution reduction costs
Property rights	Synergism
Environmental taxation	Quotas
Marketable permits	

Further reading

Burningham, D. and Davies, J., *Green Economics*, 2nd edn., Heinemann, 1999.

Griffiths, A. and Wall, S., Chapter 10 in *Applied Economics*, Pearson, 8th edn, 1999.

Munday, S., Chapter 6 in *Current Developments in Economics*, Macmillan, 1996.

Sloman, J., Chapter 12 in *Economics*, Prentice Hall, 4th edn, 2000.

Useful websites

Environment Agency: www.environment-agency.gov.uk/
The European Environment Agency: www.eea.eu.int/
Severn-Trent: www.severn-trent.com/
Friends of the Earth: www.foe.co.uk/

Essay topics

1. (a) Explain why economists regard pollution as an example of market failure. [10 marks]
   (b) How might pollution problems be dealt with through taxation? Comment upon how this approach compares with that of using legislation to control pollution. [15 marks]
   [OCR, November 1997]

2. (a) Explain why the rapid depletion of fish stocks may be considered to be an example of market failure. [40 marks]
   (b) Examine the measures which governments might take to conserve fish stock [60 marks]
   [Edexcel January 1998]

Data response question

This task is part of the Edexcel exam board's specimen paper for 2000. Study the text and the two figures, then answer the questions that follow.

A New Way of Dealing With Pollution

An auction of pollution permits in Chicago yesterday ushered in the most sophisticated, ambitious attempt so far to harness the power of the free market to reduce the negative externality caused by acid rain pollution. The permits are to produce one ton of sulphur dioxide gas – the main cause of acid rain – from a fossil fuel power station. From 1995, if any of the 110 most polluting power stations in the USA produces more pollution in a year than it has permits for, it will face large fines.

The supporters of the new system claim that it will work 'with' rather than 'against' the market. The central idea is that the market, rather than a government regulator, is best at working out the most cost-effective way of bringing down pollution. The owners of power stations can trade permits: those facing the highest costs in curbing sulphur emissions will buy; those that can clean up their act relatively cheaply will sell.

Fresh permits will be issued each year, but the numbers will decline to a level that halves sulphur dioxide emissions early in the next century. The new system of pollution control does not come into force until 1995, but the permits have begun to be issued and trading is underway.

The auctions are intended to encourage intermediaries to come in and establish an open market price rather than allow the utilities to sew things up among themselves. The auctions are also intended to allow new entrants – companies that want to run fossil fuel power stations – to buy the permits they will require. The new system should increase flexibility: fossil fuel power stations can choose between installing expensive equipment to reduce sulphur dioxide emissions, switching to cleaner fuels, or continuing to pollute and buying allowances or permits to pollute on the market.

Source: adapted from: Nicholas Schoon 'Pollution permits make a market', in *The Independent*, 30 March 1993

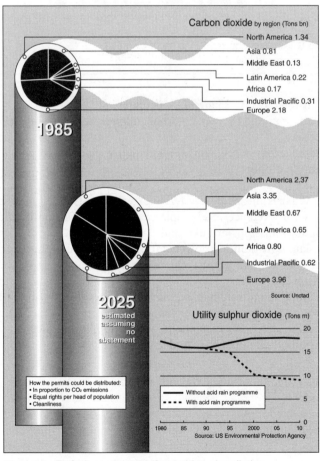

Figure A Emissions: the case for curbing air pollution

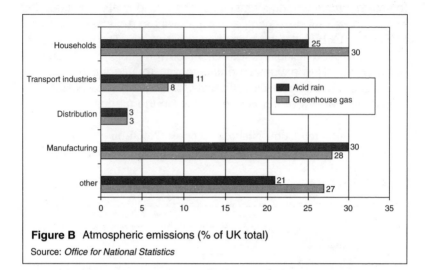

Figure B Atmospheric emissions (% of UK total)
Source: *Office for National Statistics*

1. With reference to Figure A, calculate:
   (a) the amount by which carbon dioxide emissions are expected to rise. [2 marks]
   (b) the area of the world which is expected to experience the greatest proportionate increase in carbon dioxide emissions.

   [2 marks]
2. (a) What is meant by the term 'external costs'? [2 marks]
   (b) With reference to examples explain why carbon dioxide and sulphur emissions are external costs. [6 marks]
3. Explain how granting power stations 'permits to pollute' can work 'with rather than against' the market. Illustrate your answer with a diagram. [8 marks]
4. Examine the advantages and disadvantages of reducing pollution through trading pollution permits. [10 marks]
5. Examine *two* other methods which might be used to reduce pollution from acid rain and greenhouse gases. [10 marks]

Chapter Nine

Health care

'The National Health Service is a fine institution, that given the resources and the changes necessary will once again be the pride of Britain and the envy of the world.'
Tony Blair (2000)

'If you think health care is expensive now, wait until you see what it costs when it's free'.
P.J. O'Rourke (1993)

The provision of good quality health care is seen by all of us as an important part of any developed society. We all seem to agree that a good health service is a vital aspect of our society and an appropriate use of at least some of our scarce resources. However, we all also seem to feel varying levels of satisfaction with our health service. At worst, it is seen, at least at times, to be in a state of crisis. The sort of front-page report in *The Independent* shown below has not been uncommon in recent years. It suggests clearly that all is not seen to be well with health care provision in the United Kingdom. Similar concerns are often expressed in other developed nations.

Economic theory can help us to understand the nature of the market for health care and its provision and give insights into the problems that appear to exist. The problem is an economic one. We have very many health care wants but, as always, resources are scarce relative to those wants. Difficult choices have to be made and those scarce resources need to be used in the best (most efficient) way possible. The market itself is characterised both by clear failures and by further examples of government failure as governments intervene.

This chapter considers three aspects of health care provision:

1. Market failures in the health care market.
2. Possible forms of government intervention in the health care market.
3. The crisis in the health service.

Market failures in the health care market
A free health care market can be seen to be characterised by some important market failures. It is the perceived importance of these

NHS crisis: doctors warn of 'mayhem'

Alarm at shortage of intensive care beds for New Year

Colin Brown and Cherry Norton

Tony Blair faces a crisis of confidence in the Government's handling of the NHS after doctors warned last night that a shortage of intensive care beds could cause 'mayhem' over the Millennium.

Labour Party officials have privately warned Downing Street that focus group results show the health service has overtaken transport and education as the area of greatest concern to voters. The public believes the Government is failing to deliver on its election promises to make the NHS better.

Ministers denied there was a crisis in the NHS yesterday and played down the fears raised by doctors that patients could be at risk over the severe shortage of intensive care beds in London, Liverpool and the North-West of England. But there were clear signals the problems could become more than the usual 'winter pressures'. John Hutton, the Health minister, admitted the NHS was under 'acute pressure'.

At one stage yesterday, the capital had no available intensive care beds and it was reported that the nearest was in Eastbourne. Doctors warned that seriously ill patients would have to be transported hundreds of miles for treatment which was a 'very dangerous situation' as many patients were too sick to travel long distances safely.

The Independent, 29 December 1999

market failures that explains why governments in developed countries have always been so significantly involved in the health care provision of their societies. Five main areas of market failure are considered here:

- Positive externalities of health care.
- Health care as a merit good.
- Information failures in the health care market.
- Possible monopoly power in health care provision.
- Equity concerns in health care provision.

Positive externalities

The provision of health care to any one individual or group of people may generate benefits to third parties. There may be external benefits. The nature of some health problems is that they can have an impact on others. A contagious disease can be caught by others. Thus, a vaccination that prevents a person from catching a contagious disease can benefit others who will no longer be susceptible to catching that disease themselves. The social benefits of the vaccination go beyond the private benefits. Another example might be that employers benefit when their employees receive health care and thus take less time off work.

The problem with products that generate positive externalities is that they are likely to be under-provided by the free market. This was illustrated by Figure 9 in chapter 4 (see page 34). Thus there is the likelihood that the free market will not see enough scarce resources dedicated to the provision of health care.

Health care as a merit good

At least some aspects of health care can be characterised as examples of merit goods. People are not fully aware of the true benefits to them of the health care: there is an under-valuing of health care services. This could be seen to be true with such things as **preventative medicine**. Where there is no perceived current illness or ill health, then the benefits of paying for medical services that might prevent future illness or ill health might not be clearly seen. No obvious signs of breast cancer to a person might mean that the person sees no or little benefit in having to pay for breast screening that might detect any cancer before it becomes very serious. The true benefits could be very great to the person concerned.

As with products generating positive externalities, the problem with merit goods is that they are likely to be under-provided and under-consumed in the free market. This was illustrated by Figure 10 in chapter 4 (see page 39).

Information failures

Merit goods can be seen as examples of a failure of information: consumers do not have full information about the benefits of the product and thus under-consume it. However, there are other important examples of information failures in the health care market that are likely to cause it to fail:

• The fundamental trade in health care provision involves a clear inequality in the possession of information. Why do you visit your doctor? It is usually because you do not know what is wrong with your health and you hope that your doctor will know. The essence of the relationship is one of unequal information. In a truly free, private market, consumers buy information about their state of health and suggested treatment from their doctor.

The problem with this unequal (or **asymmetric**) **information** would be if patients and doctors had different objectives. A doctor whose sole aim was to provide the best possible diagnosis and suggested treatment to every patient would have identical aims to his or her patients. Market failure should not occur. However, if a doctor could increase his or her income by recommending certain treatments (perhaps possessing an interest in a particular drug company), then interests could diverge. Patients might be advised to have a treatment that is unnecessary or inappropriate. In this case, trades that take the economy away from Pareto optimality can be seen to occur. Only one party is benefiting from the transaction.

- Problems of insurance markets. Chapter 4 explained how insurance markets could fail due to information problems leading to adverse selection. This problem was seen as being compounded by the problem of moral hazard. Given the uncertain nature of one's future health, insurance against ill health is likely to be demanded by many citizens. However, the dangers of adverse selection in a free market compounded by the problem of moral hazard may mean that such markets fail. In the worst case, they will simply not operate and thus people cannot insure themselves against future ill health.

It is interesting to note that the adverse selection problem may become even worse with the use of genetic testing as this will give individuals greater knowledge about their likely health risks than insurance companies will possess.

Monopoly power

It is possible that monopoly power may develop in health care markets. There are two principal ways in which this could occur:

- There are economies of scale available in the provision of many health services. This is particularly so with hospital provision. Unit cost of provision is likely to be lower if the hospital is larger. This implies that, especially in rural areas, there may be little or no consumer choice about which hospital can be used.
- There are a limited number of doctors. Entrance qualifications ensure a limited total number of doctors, and then, especially in smaller communities, the number of doctors who could operate in a profitable fashion would be limited. There would be little consumer choice available in terms of which doctor might be seen by a patient.

Given these monopoly possibilities, there could be the sorts of inefficiencies described in chapter 4 that are attributable to monopolies. Costs may be unnecessarily high and the service most demanded by consumers will not necessarily be provided.

Equity concerns

Chapter 5 suggested that one of the main concerns about market provision was that it could be inequitable. There might be great inequalities if everything were left to the market. This is clearly an area of concern in the health market, especially in two ways:

- Much of the demand for health services is generated simply due to someone's misfortune. They may have contracted a disease or an illness that is no fault of their own. They may have been injured in a way that they were not blameworthy. It might thus be judged as 'unfair' that people who require health services should have to pay for these to be provided while those who have the good fortune not to become ill do not have to purchase such services. There is implicitly a suggestion here that some forms of health care perhaps should be paid for if they are judged to be required due to the actions of the person concerned (perhaps participating in dangerous sports or smoking).
- There is a strong feeling amongst many in developed economies that everyone has a 'right' to a 'decent' level of health. Developed economies 'should' provide health care so that everyone can be sufficiently healthy to participate reasonably fully in society. This could never be guaranteed in a free market economy. A combination of poor health and low income would seal the fate of at least some individuals.

These are clearly significant value judgements. It is hard for economists to comment on them. However, it is the job of economists to be clear about the implications of such views for the provision of health care and the implications of that provision for the rest of the economy.

This concern over possible inequity in the health care market is clearly expressed below in *The Independent*'s report of the study *The Widening Gap* that suggested the degree of inequality in health in the United Kingdom. It indicates the extent to which health inequalities are related to income and wealth inequalities.

Government intervention in the health care market

Given the range of market failures that are present in the health care

Preventable deaths grow as health gap widens

JEREMY LAURENCE

The health gap between rich and poor in Britain is the widest on record and is continuing to grow, researchers report today.

The study, published as a book, *The Widening Gap*, is the most comprehensive since the Black Report of 1980.

For the first time, the report compares geographical areas to find the 'worst health' and 'best health' parts of Britain and reveals a clear north/south divide. If people in the worst areas had enjoyed the same health as those in the best, 71 per cent of the deaths under 65 would not have occurred between 1991 and 1995, a saving of more than 10,000 lives.

The geographical comparisons show the infant mortality rate is twice as high in Salford, one of the worst areas, as in Suffolk, one of the best, and that 7,500 infants might have been saved between 1991 and 1995 if every area had matched the rate in Suffolk.

The health gap mirrors gaps in income, education and employment levels. The average household income in Glasgow Springburn, one of the worst areas, is £13,697 compared with £24,490 in Wokingham, Berkshire. Average incomes in the worst areas are 30 per cent less than those in the best areas.

The Independent, 2 December 1999

market, there is clearly a strong case for government intervention. However, that then begs the question of what intervention should take place. Four possibilities could be the following:

1. Subsidy.
2. Regulation or codes of conduct.
3. Government provision of health care insurance.
4. Free government provision of health care.

Subsidy

It was suggested above that health care could be seen as both a product generating positive externalities and as a merit good. Chapter six suggested that the standard suggestion for a policy to deal with both such products could be the same: a subsidy.

The problem with both merit goods and products generating positive externalities is that they tend to be under-produced and under-consumed in the free market. Too few scarce resources are devoted to their production and consumption. A subsidy paid to the producer lowers the cost of production, lowers the market price and encourages a higher level of production. This is illustrated in Figure 14 in chapter 6. The main problem with this policy is setting the subsidy at the correct level. As discussed in chapter 7, the problem that governments have is their lack of information about such things. It is a policy that can be seen to be operating to some extent in the UK in the form of charges for **prescriptions** (set at £6 per prescription in 2000) that many people have to pay. This cost, on average, is significantly below the market price of the drugs received for the prescription.

Regulation or codes of conduct

Insofar as monopoly power develops in a free health care market, there is a case for government regulation as with all other forms of monopoly power. This could take the form of imposing maximum prices, as with the large privatised utilities in the UK. However, the regulation might take other forms, such as the requirement of the privatised utilities to provide a product of an acceptable quality, as judged by a regulator. This is the system in state education in the UK: the Office for Standards in Education (OFSTED) regularly inspects and reports upon all schools to ensure that a certain quality of product is being delivered. There could clearly be a case for such a system with the provision of health care.

There are similar possibilities arising from the problem of unequal knowledge between producer and consumer in the health care market. There is clearly a case for regulation to ensure that health care providers do not take advantage of their possession of knowledge. However, this is also an area that has traditionally been handled by codes of conduct in the medical profession. It is simply agreed by medical practitioners that they will not exploit their position. This is the origin of the **Hippocratic oath** formerly taken by doctors. This affirmed their obligations and proper conduct and might thus guard against any possible exploitation of patients. There is clearly debate possible about whether such **self-regulation** of the medical profession is sufficient.

Government provision of health care insurance

Given the serious failings of the market for health care insurance, there appears a strong case for government intervention in this market, perhaps implying the need for the government to provide the insurance for everyone if the free market will not do so. If the true health risks of individuals cannot properly be assessed by providers of health insurance, then the government may simply have to fund a universal health insurance system out of general taxation. This would overcome the problem of adverse selection and ensure complete coverage of all citizens.

It is important to note that such a policy does not at all have to imply the need for the government to provide health care. Health care provision could be entirely provided by the private sector but funded by the state insurance system. This could be deemed as having the merit of preserving some competition in health care provision that could encourage productive and allocative efficiency.

Free provision of health care

The greatest possible form of government intervention in the health care market is for it to take over the market completely and provide all health care and make it **free at the point of consumption**. This is the basic system of the National Health Service in the UK and the policy of many other developed nations.

The interesting point to note about free provision of health care is that it is not at all obviously suggested by the market failures that are present in the health care market. The clear case for free provision in economic theory comes from the example of public goods. These will not be produced by the private sector. However, health care is not a public good. In many ways, it is closer to a private good than a public good: it is both excludable and rival. It is provided by the private sector. There is an obvious case for its subsidy and for the need for the government to ensure that the health insurance market functions properly. However, there is no immediate suggestion that the whole market should be owned and run by the government and provided free of charge at the point that the health care is consumed. The question must thus be asked as to why this happens.

The only possible justification for the government free provision of health care is on the grounds of equity. If a certain level of health is seen as a 'right' for all citizens, then there is an argument for providing the necessary health care free of charge to the user and funding it via the tax system. This means that there will be a re-distribution from those on higher incomes to those suffering from ill health. Many developed societies have made the value judgement that this is the right thing to do.

It should be noted that for the economist there are likely to be problems with such a system. Clearly, the incentive problems over any government-run organisation discussed in chapter 7 could apply to a state-run health care service. More specifically, providing any product free of charge will lead to difficulties. A zero price is the equivalent of a very low maximum price. Standard supply and demand analysis suggests that the imposition of a maximum price on a market leads to several things:

- shortages
- queues
- black markets

As there tends to be an excess of demand over supply where the price is held below the equilibrium level then there are bound to be shortages and queues. Unofficial markets also tend to exist where price is pushed up closer to its equilibrium level. If we substitute the term 'black market' for 'private market', these characteristics can all clearly be seen to exist in the UK's health care market. As economists, we should not be surprised by shortages of beds and waiting lists.

It can further be suggested that a zero price for a product is likely to lead to an over-consumption and over-production of that product if the government attempts to meet the level of demand at the zero price. This implies allocative inefficiency.

The crisis in the health service

It is possible to begin to understand the serious difficulties of the health service in the UK and other developed countries when the likely problems of free provision are understood. There are reasons why free provision of health care has led to such acute problems. Two particular features of modern health care that are likely to lead to sharply rising demand and costs:

1. Ageing populations. Every developed country has an ageing population. This is creating ever-greater demands on health care. This is not a trend that is in any way set to stop.
2. Innovations in treatments and drugs. More and more possibilities of treating ill health are discovered and made available to society, usually at a significant cost. Such innovations (such as Viagra) create new demands and cost pressures.

With these trends it is not unreasonable to see demand at a zero price as virtually unlimited. As economists, we know that unlimited desires always come up against the problem of scarce resources. Difficult decisions have to be made about what to produce and what not to produce. In a free market, the market price sorts out this problem. In the health care market there have to be alternatives. Different ways of rationing the supply of health care have to be found.

The article below from *The Daily Telegraph* makes it clear how rationing takes place in one particular **Health Authority**. The truth is that rationing must always take place: it is simply a matter of how.

The answer of the West Hertfordshire Health Authority to the problem of how to allocate scarce resources in the absence of a price system is to draw up lists of what treatments can and cannot be

Hospital chiefs admit to rationing surgery

CELIA HALL and MICHAEL SMITH

A health authority has admitted that it is operating a ban on a number of specific drugs and surgical procedures, including treatment for patients dying of cancer.

West Hertfordshire Health Authority is also refusing fertility treatment and cholesterol-reducing drugs. The authority, based in St Albans, claimed its '**Low Priority Treatment Policy**' – which lists 32 operations and treatments that it will not provide except in extreme circumstances – was not based on the treatments' costs and that very few patients had complained.

But Kerry Pollard, MP for St Albans, said he was astonished that the authority felt it had to refuse treatment to people dying of cancer. He said: 'That doesn't sound like a low-priority case to me. It is an appalling situation. People suffering from cancer should be allowed to die with dignity. It is very disappointing if people are being refused cancer treatment, particularly when Frank Dobson, the Health Secretary, has said there is £21 billion of new

money available for the Health Service.'

West Hertfordshire Health Authority is unusual for not being afraid to admit that it is rationing treatment. In a statement it said: 'Rationing of some kind has always been part of the NHS. Waiting lists are a form of rationing. The difference is that the process is now much more open and transparent.'

The authority is facing a deficit of £6.5 million on its £300 million budget. But Dr Barry Tennison, the authority's director of public health, said the Low Priority Treatment Policy was based more on the effectiveness of the treatments than on their costs. Dr Tennison said: 'There has been surprisingly little adverse reaction from patients. We believe in being explicit. The more open we are the more they will understand the hard decisions we have to make.'

Dr Tennison said most health authorities were likely to 'have a piece of paper' that set out priorities but West Hertfordshire was unusual in having a carefully-formed five-page policy.

The Daily Telegraph, 1 August 1998

provided. This clearly means that there is unsatisfied demand at zero price and thus that there is likely to be dissatisfaction, as expressed by the local MP.

An alternative way of trying to ration health care in the absence of the operation of the price system is to give treatments that represent the 'best value' or are most efficient. This can be measured in terms of the expenditure required on the treatment relative to the level of benefit received by the patient. The treatments with the greatest ratio of benefit to cost are those that should take priority. This is what the system of 'QALYs' attempts to do. QALYs stands for **Quality of Life Years**. All treatments can be judged in terms of how much they improve life multiplied by the number of years that the improved quality is enjoyed. This level of measured benefit can then be compared with the cost of each treatment to draw up a league table of different treatments in terms of how good a use of scarce resources that they represent.

Long-term worries

Clearly, there is scope for the private sector to play a part in health care. In particular, competing private firms may be the most efficient **providers of health services.** What role private insurance should play is harder to judge. If, as seems likely, public funding will continue to be the main pillar, ways must be found to give the public more influence over how much is spent, and on what.

At present, the main, sledgehammer, option is to vote out a government in a general election. One promising possibility is to hand the health budget to a separate institution, run by officials elected by the public to do only that job, and funded by a hypothecated tax raised only for that purpose. This might give voters more of a choice. More debate about which health services the government will pay for – correction of unequal leg lengths? Heart transplants? Viagra? – might also be welcome. But as long as most voters think of health care as a free good available in unlimited quantity, and politicians encourage them in that belief, nothing will change for the better.

The Economist, 24 October 1998

If the health service is in a crisis, we are left with the question of what is the best way forward. *The Economist* article above suggests that turning towards more private provision may be the best solution although it is unclear precisely what system might be wanted. There are clear benefits:

- Competition among health care providers may raise efficiency.
- Charging for health care makes consumers consider what is and what is not valuable health care for them.
- The problems of shortages, queues and two-tier systems might be improved.

However, there are two major problems with making such a move towards the private sector:

- The inefficiencies due to the various market failures will become stronger.
- The system may be judged to be inequitable. People on low incomes will not be able to afford much health care. Those suffering from ill health will find that much of their income is devoted to health treatment.

One of the major government failures suggested in chapter 7 must also be recalled. If politicians seek above all else to be re-elected, then the possibility that a government will clearly move away from a system of the principle of universal free health care seems remote. Such a move might be seen as a major vote-loser and thus not countenanced by vote-maximising politicians. The system of ever-increasing expenditure and ever-increasing frustration with the health service seems the most likely possibility. There are no easy answers in this complicated market.

KEY WORDS

Preventative medicine	Prescriptions
Asymmetric information	Hippocratic oath
National Health Service	Self-regulation
Ageing population	Free at the point of
Medical innovations	consumption
Pooling of risks	Health authority
Budget cap	Low Priority Treatment Policy
Health care rationing	Quality of Life Years (QALYs)
Health care providers	

Further reading

Atkinson, B. *et al.*, Chapter 10 in *Applied Economics*, Macmillan, 1998.

Griffiths, A. and Wall, S., Chapter 13 in *Applied Economics*, Pearson, 8th edn, 1999.

Munday, S., Chapter 7 in *Current Developments in Economics*, Macmillan, 1996.

Parkin, M. *et al.*, Chapter 17 in *Economics*, 4th edn., Addison Wesley, 2000.

Useful websites
Department of Health: www.doh.gov.uk/
World Health Organisation: www.who.org/

Essay topics
1. (a) The basic economic problem which confronts every society is scarcity. Explain how, in a market economy, the price mechanism allocates resources between different cases.   [12 marks]
   (b) Evaluate the arguments for and against a significant reduction in the state provision of health care, which results in an increase in the supply of health care through the market mechanism.
                                                                        [13 marks]
2. In most countries the role of the state in the economy has been reduced in recent years.
   (a) Analyse the factors which might explain this trend. [50 marks]
   (b) Examine the likely economic implications of an increase in the proportion of health care and education provided by the private sector.   [50 marks]
   [Edexcel, June 1999]

Data response question
This task is based on a question set by the AQA exam board for its Market Failure specimen paper for 2000. Study the table and extracts, and then answer the questions that follow:

Table A Selected areas of UK general government expenditure In real terms

	£ billion at 1996 prices			
	1981	1986	1991	1996
Social security	64	80	85	107
Health	28	31	36	43
Education	29	31	34	39
Defence	26	30	27	23
Housing and community amenities	15	13	10	10
All other expenditure	241	259	264	306

Source: *Social Trends*, 1998

Extract A

The demand for health care appears to constantly rise from year to year. Demographic changes in the population relentlessly increase the need for health care and, on top of this, we have a nation where average real incomes have been rising over a long period of time, and which demand better health care for its money. Governments have been spending more each year in real terms but demand has persistently outpaced the supply of services, such that the National Health Service (NHS) has suffered from a severe dose of under-funding.

Extract B

In 1947, the National Health Service boldly attempted to get rid of the connection between access to health care and the ability to pay. This system has failed because of the removal of health care from the market place. If a commodity is offered free at the point of consumption there will be excess demand; some rationing device must be found. The NHS uses several; some patients are not treated, some join waiting lists or go private, and more urgent cases are treated according to informal and often arbitrary priority schemes. Not only does this cause inefficiency in the allocation of resources but it also is a cause of constant political embarrassment; the Government is blamed for waiting lists and particular failures of treatment, as recently we have seen with children in intensive care and the constant claims by doctors of the inadequacy of resources.

In fact, the NHS has failed because there is no competition to spur producers into better efforts, and because the consumer has no say in the allocation of resources. Efficiency has been the loser.

Economic efficiency and political considerations both point to a greater role for the market, with government intervention reserved to ensure effective protection of the weak and the poor.

Source: adapted from Patrick Minford, *Economic Affairs*, October–November 1998

Extract C
Selling off doctors

Much nonsense is spoken about the provision of health care through the market system. Certain basic principles need to be established.

1. A GP who is attending to a private patient cannot at the same time be treating an NHS patient.
2. People who pay money to go to doctors whom they could see for free on the NHS do so for only one purpose: to jump the queue.
3. Jumping the queue means getting access to health care not according to how sick you are but according to your bank balance.
4. The British NHS is the best health care system in the world because it is based on production for use and not profit and because it treats patients according to their health not wealth. It is far more efficient and fairer at every level than the health care system in the United States where people are treated according to their wealth.

Source: adapted from *The Guardian*, 12 January 1999

1. Using Table A, compare the change in government expenditure on health with the change in other areas of government expenditure between 1981 and 1996. [5 marks]
2. Using Extract A and your knowledge of economics:
   (a) state *four* factors which may have caused the demand for health care to rise; [4 marks]
   (b) explain how *two* of these factors have contributed to the increase in demand for health care in the UK. [6 marks]
3. Discuss the advantages and disadvantages of the government charging NHS patients for the services they receive. [20 marks]

Conclusion

The purpose of this book has been to examine some fundamental areas of economic theory and to consider how they can be appropriately applied to a number of important current issues. It is hoped that the reader has both appreciated the theory and seen how it has much relevant application.

There may be various key points that any reader will take away from examining this area of economics. The following could well be some of them:

- Markets can be very powerful. They can and often do achieve the fundamental problem of how to allocate our scarce resources in the best fashion.
- It cannot be guaranteed that markets will always work well. There are several important reasons why they may sometimes lead to undesirable allocations and uses of scarce resources.
- There is certainly a theoretical case for governments intervening in markets that are not working well to try to improve resource allocation and use in those markets. The problem, however, is that governments, even if well-intentioned, may not improve the situation. There is even a chance that they could make things worse.
- Major issues in our society today can be better understood with an appreciation of the relevant economics. How can we really say whether governments should or should not get involved in particular situations? How can we judge whether one type of government policy is likely to be more successful and appropriate than another? The answer is by studying the relevant economics and thinking carefully about its proper application.

Perhaps the most important message of this book is that economics is not just a subject of academic enquiry to be confined to the classroom, lecture hall and library. It is a subject that can have real application to the world in which we live and help us to understand and appreciate some of the important issues of the day.

Index